"Robin Benzle's style is lighthearted and irreverent, while our beloved hero's creator, Tom Wilson, plays with your head -- and heart. Their book is packed with old-fashioned/new-twist recipes that are homey, good-sounding or just loony enough to make you want to try 'em. And try 'em again.

THE ZIGGY COOKBOOK shows it's OK to play with your food. You can't help but talk with your mouth full........about this book."

-JOE CREA, FOOD EDITOR
The Orange County Register

THE ZiGGY® COOKBOOK
GREAT FOOD FROM
MOM'S DINER

Also by Robin Benzle:

COOKING WITH HUMOR: A UNIQUE RECIPE COLLECTION

THE ZiGGY® COOKBOOK
GREAT FOOD FROM
MOM'S DINER

by ROBIN BENZLÉ with illustrations by Tom Wilson

VANTINE PUBLISHING COMPANY
COOKBOOK PUBLISHERS
BAY VILLAGE, OHIO

PUBLISHER'S CATALOGING IN PUBLICATION
(Prepared by Quality Books Inc.)

Benzle, Robin Copper.
    The Ziggy cookbook: great food from Mom's Diner / by Robin Benzle
with illustrations by Tom Wilson.
    p. cm.
    Includes index.
    ISBN 0-9629398-2-X

    1. Cookery. 2. Ziggy (Cartoon character) I. Wilson, Tom,
ill. II. Title.

TX714.B39Z5 1993   641.5
                                    QB193-1046

Library of Congress Catalog Card Number: 93-60839

Dedicated to my Mom and Dad.
The weather's beautiful. Wish you were here.

Love,

Robin

CONTENTS

CHAPTER 15 - DIXIE FIXINS'

CHAPTER 16 - THE POT ROAST CHAPTER

CHAPTER 17 - MOM'S APPLE PIES

CHAPTER 18 - MOM'S WORLD TOUR

PROPER THANK YOU NOTES TO:

Charles Schultz
Lynn Johnston
Mort Walker
John Saunders and Joe Giella
Jim Davis
Tom Batiuk and Chuck Ayers
Roger Bollen
Dean Young and Stan Drake
Johnny Hart and Brant Parker
Chris Browne
Jim Unger
King Features Syndicate
Universal Press Syndicate
Creators Syndicate
United Feature Syndicate
Eric Benzle
Arthur and Martha Benzle
Bailey and Erin Benzle
Mary Eitzen
Sue Dreher
Jeanne Csoltko
Caroline Kennemuth
Cynthia Deering
Charles M. Gentile
Margaret Noonan Blaum
Sally Kamman
Elizabeth Parsell
Tom Thornton
Eric Bruce

...I'M NOT GONNA GET ALL MUSHY...BUT MANY THANKS TO ALL THESE GREAT FOLKS FOR BRINGING MY CARTOON DINER TO LIFE!

A WORD FROM MOM...

Welcome to Mom's Diner. For over 20 years my Diner has been Ziggy's favorite eatery. Here, you're guaranteed mouth-watering, lip-smacking, belly-warming food served up most often with a little motherly advice and a lot of napkins.

One day, my friend Ziggy convinced me that the time had come to reveal my secrets and share some of my personal recipes with you, so here are about 160 of them, with my blessings. You'll see some nostalgic dishes mixed in with my newest inventions. From all around America to distant shores of faraway places, there's surely something to please everyone; whether it's a Sunday morning breakfast on the back porch or a special dinner for when out of town company comes. No special equipment is needed, although I often use my favorite big, black skillet; well-seasoned wooden spoons; a good set of knives (always sharpened, of course); and I can't seem to live without that new-fangled food processor.

Now listen up, because when it comes to eating, my philosophy consists of two very important beliefs:

First, eat plenty of fresh fruits, crisp vegetables and wholesome grains, and do something physical every day, like taking a nice, brisk walk with someone that has interesting things to say. It's good for the body.

Secondly, every now and then have a nice, big helping of comfort food like Twelve Oaks Southern Fried Chicken with Cream Gravy, Twice-Baked Sweet Potatoes with Marshmallows and a warm slice of Apple Shoofly Pie; or a plate of Tom's Good Old Pot Roast with Homemade Noodles and a thick slice of stick-to-your-fork Chocolate Malt Devil's Food Cake washed down with a cup of steaming coffee with real cream. It's good for the soul.

So, come on in (wipe your feet first), pull up a stool and I'll take your order. No reservations necessary.

Chapter 1

MORNING AT MOM'S

From muffins to 'maters greet the sunrise with
nine of my most delicious breakfast offerings.
Mix and match as you see fit.

WAKE–UP COFFEE OATMEAL MUFFINS

Extra moist and studded with dates - no need to smear butter on these!

Makes 12

    3/4 cup flour
      2 teaspoons baking powder
    1/2 teaspoon salt
      1 cup quick-cooking oatmeal (not instant)
      2 tablespoons instant coffee dissolved in 1/2 cup warm water
      2 tablespoons butter or margarine, melted
    1/2 cup sugar
      1 egg, beaten
    1/2 cup chopped, dried dates

Preheat oven to 400 degrees. Grease a 12-count muffin tin. In one medium bowl, combine flour, baking powder, salt and oatmeal. In another medium bowl, combine coffee, butter, sugar and egg. Slowly pour coffee mixture into flour mixture, stirring constantly, just until blended. Do not overmix. Fold in dates. Fill muffin cups two-thirds full. Bake 15 minutes. That's all there is to it.

21

SCRAMBLED EGG CUPCAKES with CHEDDAR FROSTING

Toasted bread "baskets" filled with seasoned eggs and
topped with melted cheese. Eat them with your fingers!

Serves 4 (two each)

Baskets: 8 slices white bread, crusts removed*
2 tablespoons butter or margarine, softened

Eggs: 2 tablespoons butter or margarine
7 eggs, beaten
3 tablespoons chopped, fresh chives
(or 1 1/2 teaspoons dried)

8 squares sharp Cheddar cheese, about 2"

Preheat oven to 350 degrees. Flatten bread slices with a rolling pin. Spread butter on one side of each slice. Press bread, buttered side down, into muffin tins. Bake 12 - 15 minutes, or until lightly toasted.

While bread baskets are baking, make eggs. Melt butter in a large skillet, add eggs and chives, and cook over medium-low heat until soft-scrambled. You can season with a little salt if you like.

When bread baskets are done, turn oven temperature to 475 degrees. Fill baskets with scrambled eggs, top each with a square of Cheddar cheese and return to oven for about two minutes, or until cheese melts.

*Save the bread crusts for the next trip to the duck pond.

LEMON-LIME FRENCH TOAST
Thick, golden slices - speckled with
citrus rind and sweetened with syrup.

Makes 10

4 - 5 eggs
2 tablespoons light cream
1 tablespoon + 1 teaspoon grated lemon rind
2 tablespoons grated lime rind
Pinch black pepper
1 loaf uncut Italian bread
Butter or margarine for cooking
Maple syrup

Preheat oven to 200 degrees (to keep French toast warm later). In medium bowl (to accommodate a bread slice), whisk eggs. Stir in cream, grated rinds and pepper. Slice bread in 1" thick slices, saving end pieces for the birds.

Melt about 3 tablespoons butter in large skillet. Dip bread slices in egg mixture and fry in hot butter until golden brown, turning once. Add more butter if necessary. Remove to a baking pan and keep warm in oven until all are done. Top with maple syrup.

MUSTARD-BROILED HAM STEAKS with APPLES

Tangy mustard, salty ham and sweet apples - a perfect
trio of flavors, enhanced by a sprinkling of cloves.

Serves 6

2 ham steaks, 1/2" thick (about 1 1/2 pounds total)
4 tablespoons prepared brown mustard, total
1/2 teaspoon ground cloves, total
2 small red Delicious apples, cored, peeled and thinly sliced

Preheat oven to broil. Place ham steaks on baking sheet and spread tops with mustard, using 1 tablespoon. Sprinkle with 1/4 teaspoon of cloves. Broil 5 - 7 minutes or until lightly browned. Remove from oven and turn over. Spread remaining mustard on, sprinkle with remaining cloves, and arrange apple slices on top. Return to oven and broil 5 - 7 minutes more, or until apples are lightly browned. Cut into serving portions.

APRICOT MAPLE GRANOLA

Nutty, crunchy - always great to have on hand.

Makes about 15 cups

7 cups old-fashioned oats
1 1/2 cups wheat germ
1 cup flaked coconut
1 cup unsalted sunflower seeds
1 cup chopped walnuts, unsalted

1 cup chopped almonds, unsalted
1 teaspoon ground cinnamon
1 teaspoon salt
1 cup maple syrup
2 teaspoons vanilla extract
2 cups chopped, dried apricots (about 3/4 pound)

Preheat oven to 300 degrees. Lightly oil two baking sheets with sides. In a very large bowl or kettle, combine everything but the last three ingredients.

In a small bowl, whisk together maple syrup and vanilla extract and pour over oat mixture. Toss well.

Spread granola on prepared pans. Bake 45 minutes or until coconut is lightly browned, stirring every 15 minutes to avoid burning. Let cool and sprinkle with apricot pieces. Store in air-tight container at room temperature.

BUTTERMILK-PECAN FLAPJACKS with ORANGE SYRUP
So light and fluffy you'll be tempted to eat the entire stack.

Makes 20

1/2 teaspoon baking soda
1 cup buttermilk
1 cup milk
3 eggs, separated
4 tablespoons butter or margarine, melted
1 1/2 cups flour
1 teaspoon baking powder

1 teaspoon sugar
1 teaspoon salt
3/4 cup chopped pecans
Vegetable oil for the griddle

In a medium bowl, dissolve the baking soda in the buttermilk. Stir in milk, egg yolks, and butter. In a large bowl, combine flour, baking powder, sugar and salt. Slowly pour buttermilk mixture into flour mixture, stirring until smooth. In yet another bowl, beat egg whites until stiff and fold those in. Stir in pecans. Drop batter by large spoonfuls onto hot, lightly oiled griddle and cook over medium heat until golden brown, flipping once. Keep warm in low oven until all are done, remembering to reoil the griddle. Serve with pads of butter and warm orange syrup:

ORANGE SYRUP

Makes 2 cups

1 cup sweet butter
1 can (6 ounces) orange juice concentrate
1 cup sugar

In medium saucepan, combine all ingredients. Cook over low heat until butter is melted, stirring occasionally. Don't let it boil. You can store it in the refrigerator for several weeks, but remember to reheat it slowly.

APPLE KNOCKER SAUSAGE BALLS
Savory, seasoned pork meatballs glazed in apple juice.

Makes 20 (good for 4-6 people)

4 slices bacon, frozen (easier to chop that way)
1 teaspoon ground thyme
1/2 teaspoon ground sage
1/2 teaspoon ground mace
1 teaspoon white pepper
1/2 teaspoon dry mustard
1/4 teaspoon salt
2 cloves garlic, minced
1 pound ground pork
2 cups apple juice

In a food processor using steel blade, process bacon until finely chopped. Mix in all spices. Add pork and carefully mix without turning it mushy. Form mixture into golf ball-sized balls and place in large skillet. Cover sausage balls with apple juice. Bring to boil, and cook over medium heat, uncovered, 25 - 30 minutes, or until glazed and lightly browned.

CHICKEN COOP HASH BROWNS

Peppery, ground chicken with grated potatoes, fried until crispy.

Serves 6

2 tablespoons butter or margarine
2 tablespoons vegetable oil
1 pound lean ground chicken
4 scallions, sliced (include a little green)
2 1/4 pounds potatoes, grated (about 4 good-sized Idahos)
1 1/2 teaspoons salt
1 teaspoon black pepper
1 teaspoon white pepper

In large skillet (wrought iron is good for this one), heat butter and oil. Add ground chicken and cook over medium-low heat, breaking up with a fork, until no longer pink. Mix in scallions and cook 1 minute more. Let cool slightly and remove to a large bowl. Stir in potatoes, salt and both peppers. Add a little more vegetable oil to same skillet, and add potato mixture, spreading to cover bottom. Flatten with the back of a metal spatula, and cook over medium heat until bottom is nicely browned. Cut into sixths and turn each piece to brown second side.

MOM'S MORNING 'MATERS

*Broiled cream cheese-topped tomato halves -
a perfect companion to eggs in any form.*

Serves 8

8 ounces cream cheese, softened
1 tablespoon sherry
1 tablespoon cream (light or heavy)
1 tablespoon minced onion
1/4 teaspoon salt
2 tablespoons chopped, fresh parsley
4 decent-sized tomatoes, halved
1/2 cup fresh bread crumbs

Preheat oven to broil. In medium bowl, blend together with a fork, cream cheese, sherry, cream, onion, salt and parsley. Trim bottoms of tomatoes to lie flat, if you need to. Place on baking sheet, cut side up, and top with cream cheese mixture. Sprinkle bread crumbs over. Broil in lower third of oven until crumbs are browned and cheese is bubbly, about 6 - 8 minutes.

Chapter 2

SOUP FOR WHAT AILS 'YA

Whether it's a case of the blues, or an oncoming cold, there's something soothing about soup. Hot or cold, hearty or light, surely there's one here to comfort you.

CHICKEN SOUP with HOMEMADE PARSLEY NOODLES

Cider vinegar adds pizzazz and the noodles are
simply poured in - almost like mini dumplings.

Serves 8 - 10, sniffles or no sniffles

3 tablespoons butter or margarine
2 cups coarsely chopped onion (about 2 medium)
2 cups chopped celery (about 4 stalks)
3 quarts (12 cups) chicken stock or broth
2 cups diced carrots (about 1/2 pound)
2 1/2 pounds boneless, skinless chicken breast, cut into
bite-sized pieces
3 tablespoons cider vinegar
3/4 teaspoon pepper
1/2 teaspoon dried oregano

Noodles: 4 eggs
1/2 cup flour
1/2 cup chopped, fresh parsley
1 teaspoon salt

In a large soup kettle, melt butter over medium heat and cook onions until golden. Stir in celery, cook 1 minute more. Add stock and carrots, and bring to a boil. Add chicken, cider vinegar, pepper and oregano and simmer 40 minutes, covered (scrape off any foam that forms on the top).

Make noodle batter: In medium bowl, beat eggs. Slowly add flour, then parsley and salt. Very slowly pour batter into soup. In a few minutes, small noodles will appear. Saltines are my cracker of choice.

SPAGHETTI and MEATBALL SOUP

*A guaranteed favorite for all ages. Serve it with a soup
spoon and a fork to more easily lasso those noodles.*

Serves 8

Meatballs:
    1 1/2 pounds ground sirloin
    1/2 pound ground pork
    1 egg
    1/2 cup fine, dry bread crumbs
    3 - 4 cloves garlic, minced
    1 teaspoon salt
    1/2 teaspoon pepper
    1 tablespoon fresh, chopped oregano leaves
    (or 1 teaspoon dried)

Soup:
    1 1/2 quarts (6 cups) beef stock or broth
    1 1/2 cups water
    28 ounce can crushed tomatoes
    1/3 cup grated Parmesan cheese (canned)
    1/2 teaspoon dried rosemary leaves, crushed
    1/2 teaspoon dried basil leaves
    2/3 pound spaghetti noodles, broken in half

In large bowl, mix all meatball ingredients together with hands. Form into 1" balls and place in large, deep skillet. Pour water over to almost cover. Cook over medium-high heat, turning, until done, 12 - 15 minutes. Drain liquid.

Meanwhile, make soup: In large kettle, place beef broth, water, tomatoes (include juice), cheese, rosemary and basil. Bring to a boil, lower heat, and simmer 20 minutes, uncovered. Add meatballs, bring to a boil, and add noodles. Simmer until noodles are tender, stirring occasionally, about 10 minutes.

Serve with big chunks of garlic bread.

PUMPKIN PATCH PEANUT BUTTER SOUP

Savory and soothing on a blustery autumn afternoon.

Serves 8

3 tablespoons butter or margarine
1/2 cup minced onion (1 small onion)
4 cups cooked pumpkin (canned is fine)
3 cups chicken stock or broth
1/3 cup smooth peanut butter
1/4 teaspoon cayenne pepper
1 teaspoon salt
1/2 teaspoon ground nutmeg
2 cups light cream or half and half
Chives for a little color

In a soup pot over medium heat, melt butter and cook onions until soft, about 5 minutes. Lower heat, add pumpkin, stock, peanut butter, cayenne, salt and nutmeg, and cook, stirring until peanut butter is melted. Stir in cream and warm through, without boiling. Sprinkle with chives.

CREAM OF MUSHROOM SOUP with ALMONDS

Ground almonds add texture and flavor to an already terrific soup.

Serves 6

WELL, BABY...
LOOKS LIKE WE'RE
IN THIS THING
TOGETHER...

...WELL,
PERSONALLY
I THINK WE'RE
GONNA GET
CREAMED!

4 tablespoons butter or margarine
1 small onion, finely chopped
1 pound mushrooms, trimmed and coarsely chopped
4 tablespoons flour
2 cups chicken stock or broth
1 cup finely ground blanched almonds (no skins)
1 tablespoon lemon juice
2 cups light cream or half and half
1 tablespoon chopped fresh thyme leaves (or 1/2
    teaspoon dried)
1/4 teaspoon ground nutmeg
1 teaspoon salt
1/2 teaspoon ground white pepper

In a large soup pot, melt butter over medium heat. Add onion and mushrooms and cook, stirring, until vegetables are softened, about 5 minutes. Lower heat, stir in flour and cook 2 minutes more. Add chicken stock, almonds and lemon juice, bring to a simmer and cook 5 minutes. Add light cream, thyme and remaining spices and heat through without boiling. Oyster crackers are a nice complement.

CORN CHOWDER with SCALLOPS

Hearty, creamy chowder crowded with tender scallops that
would make any sea captain happy during the foulest of storms.

AYEE MATEY!

Serves 6 - 8

4 slices bacon, chopped
1 medium onion, chopped
4 large potatoes, peeled and diced
2 packages (10 ounce) frozen corn kernels, thawed (or
    4 cups fresh)
2 cups milk
1/4 cup butter or margarine
2 teaspoons salt
1/2 teaspoon ground white pepper
1 teaspoon sugar
1 pound bay scallops (the smaller type)
1 cup heavy cream

In a large pot with a lid, cook bacon over medium-low heat until browned. Add onion and cook 1 minute more. Stir in potatoes and 1 1/2 cups water, cover, and simmer until potatoes are tender, about 10 minutes. Add corn, milk, butter, salt, pepper and sugar. Cover again and simmer another 20 minutes. Add bay scallops, and cook 4 - 5 more minutes. Just before serving, add cream and heat through without boiling. Serve with chunks of dark rye bread.

STEAK 'n TATER SOUP

Belly-warming meat and potatoes in a tomato-beef broth
with a little zucchini for good measure.

Serves 8

4 tablespoons butter or margarine
1 pound (about 3 small) zucchini, sliced and cut into bite-sized pieces
1 large onion, chopped
1 1/2 pounds steak (rib or sirloin is good), cut into 1/2" pieces
4 large potatoes (about 2 1/2 pounds), peeled and diced
6 cups beef stock or broth
15 ounce can tomato sauce or puree
1/2 teaspoon dried thyme leaves (or 1 tablespoon fresh)
1 1/2 teaspoons salt
1 teaspoon pepper
1/4 teaspoon sugar
Freshly grated Parmesan cheese

In a large soup pot, melt butter and cook zucchini until softened and starting to brown. Remove with slotted spoon to a bowl. Add onion to soup pot and cook until soft. Add steak pieces and cook until browned. Stir in beef stock, tomato sauce, thyme, salt, pepper and sugar. Bring to a simmer, add potatoes and cook, uncovered 20 minutes, or until potatoes are tender. Return zucchini to pot and simmer 5 minutes more. Top each serving with freshly grated cheese.

Divide any steak scraps between the dog and the cat.

BLT SOUP

Bacon, leek, and tomato. A swell way to use those plump garden tomatoes and fresh herbs. Freeze for winter.

Serves 6

1/2 pound bacon
2 large leeks, washed thoroughly and trimmed, leaving just a little green
6 - 8 fresh, ripe tomatoes, quartered
2 1/2 cups chicken stock or broth
1 tablespoon chopped, fresh basil leaves (or 1/2 teaspoon dried)
1 tablespoon chopped, fresh thyme leaves (or 1/2 teaspoon dried)
1/4 teaspoon sugar
1/2 teaspoon salt
1/4 teaspoon ground white pepper
1/4 cup tomato paste
1/2 cup heavy cream

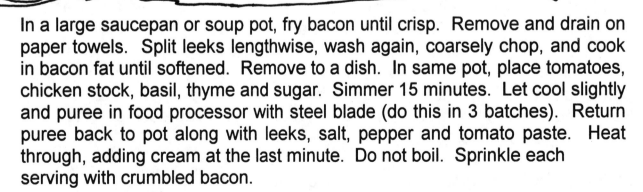

In a large saucepan or soup pot, fry bacon until crisp. Remove and drain on paper towels. Split leeks lengthwise, wash again, coarsely chop, and cook in bacon fat until softened. Remove to a dish. In same pot, place tomatoes, chicken stock, basil, thyme and sugar. Simmer 15 minutes. Let cool slightly and puree in food processor with steel blade (do this in 3 batches). Return puree back to pot along with leeks, salt, pepper and tomato paste. Heat through, adding cream at the last minute. Do not boil. Sprinkle each serving with crumbled bacon.

CHEDDAR CHEESE SOUP with BRUSSEL SPROUTS and BACK BACON

Light and cheesy. Brussels sprouts never tasted better.

Serves 4 - 6

1 pound fresh Brussels sprouts, trimmed and quartered
4 tablespoons butter or margarine
1 small onion, finely chopped
1/3 pound back bacon (Canadian bacon), cut into matchsticks
3 tablespoons flour
1 cup chicken stock or broth
2 cups milk
1/4 teaspoon dry mustard
1 teaspoon Worcestershire sauce
1/4 teaspoon pepper
2 cups shredded sharp Cheddar cheese

Microwave Brussels sprouts in a little water about 6 minutes on high. Set aside.

Melt butter in soup pot and cook onion until softened. Add bacon and cook 2 minutes. Lower heat, stir in flour and cook 1 minute. Add stock and milk and bring to a simmer. Add Brussels sprouts and cook 10 minutes until liquid is slightly thickened. Stir in mustard, Worcestershire, pepper and cheese and when the cheese is melted, it's ready.

CHICKEN-GARBANZO BEAN SOUP
with PARMESAN CHEESE

Loaded with chick peas and tiny pasta - with a whisper of sage.

BEAN SOUP-$1.50
BEEN SOUP- .45¢

Serves 5 - 6

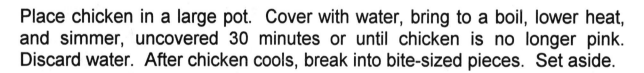

1 1/2 pounds boneless, skinless chicken breast (thighs are good, too)
6 cups chicken stock or broth
2 cups chopped celery
1 cup rosa marina pasta (or other very small type)
2 cans (16 ounces each) garbanzo beans, drained
1 teaspoon salt
1 teaspoon lemon pepper
1/4 teaspoon ground sage
Freshly grated Parmesan cheese

Place chicken in a large pot. Cover with water, bring to a boil, lower heat, and simmer, uncovered 30 minutes or until chicken is no longer pink. Discard water. After chicken cools, break into bite-sized pieces. Set aside.

In same pot, put chicken stock. Bring to a simmer and add celery and pasta. Cook over low heat, uncovered, 15 minutes. Add garbanzo beans, chicken pieces, salt, lemon pepper and sage, and simmer 5 minutes more. Top each bowlful with plenty of cheese. Bread sticks are perfect on the side.

COLD APRICOT-SOUR CREAM SOUP
Creamy, refreshing, practically a dessert.

Serves 6

1 1/2 cups dried apricots
1/2 cup sugar
1 teaspoon lemon juice
1/4 teaspoon ground nutmeg (fresh, if possible)
1 cup sour cream
1/4 cup milk

Bring 3 cups water to a boil in a medium saucepan. Add apricots and simmer 5 minutes or until tender. Drain apricots, reserving 1 1/2 cups of the cooking water. Return reserved cooking water to saucepan. Add sugar and lemon juice. Bring to a boil and cook 3 minutes or until sugar is dissolved. Let cool.

Place sugar-water in food processor with steel blade. Add apricots and nutmeg, and process until smooth. Transfer to medium bowl. When it is completely cool, whisk in sour cream and milk. Refrigerate at least one hour before serving. Small portions are plenty.

Chapter 3

THE SALAD BAR

An array of scrumptious salads that would make any rabbit happy.

BOSTON LETTUCE with WARM GARLIC BUTTER

*Unusual, and it couldn't be simpler. Goes with
just about every main course you can think of.*

Serves 6

2 heads Boston lettuce
1/2 cup freshly grated Parmesan cheese
6 tablespoons sweet butter
2 - 3 cloves garlic, peeled and halved
1 teaspoon sugar
1/2 teaspoon salt
1/2 teaspoon freshly ground black pepper

Rinse lettuce in cold water. Tear into bite-sized pieces,
wrap in a tea towel, and refrigerate.

Arrange chilled lettuce on individual salad plates.
Sprinkle each with Parmesan cheese.

In a small skillet over medium-low heat, melt butter. Add garlic, sugar, salt
and pepper and stir just until garlic starts to brown. Remove garlic pieces
and discard. Pour hot garlic butter over lettuce and serve right away.

CUCUMBER-APPLE CIDER SALAD
Tart and satisfying on a steamy, summer day.

Serves 6

3 cucumbers, peeled
1/2 cup coarsely chopped red onion
1/2 cup apple cider
3 tablespoons white vinegar
1/4 teaspoon salt
1/4 teaspoon pepper
1/2 teaspoon sugar
1/2 cup fresh parsley, chopped

Halve cucumbers lengthwise and remove seeds with a spoon. Discard seeds. Thinly slice cucumbers and place in a large, glass bowl along with onions.

In a small bowl, whisk together cider, vinegar, salt, pepper, sugar and parsley. Pour over cucumber mixture and toss. Cover and refrigerate 1 hour, but not more than 3. Toss again before serving.

STEAK 'n EGG SALAD on GREENS with ROQUEFORT DRESSING

*There's the whole meal, right there -
save for a corn muffin or two.*

...WHO SAYS SALADS HAVE TO BE "WIMPY?"

Serves 4 - 6

Dressing:
2/3 cup olive oil
3 tablespoons freshly squeezed lemon juice
1 clove garlic, minced
1 tablespoon Worcestershire sauce
4 ounces Roquefort (or other blue) cheese

Blend all ingredients in a food processor with a steel blade. Refrigerate.

Salad:
2 tablespoons butter or margarine
2 tablespoons vegetable oil
2 beef loin strip steaks (about 1 1/4 pounds), trimmed
of all fat, cut into thin strips 1" long
1 red or yellow bell pepper, cut into strips
1/2 teaspoon salt
1/2 teaspoon freshly ground black pepper
1 small head romaine lettuce, torn into bite-sized pieces
1/4 head iceberg lettuce, cut into bite-sized pieces
4 hard-boiled eggs, quartered

Heat butter and oil in medium skillet. Add steak and stir-fry 5 - 7 minutes. Add bell pepper, salt and pepper and cook 3 - 5 minutes more, until peppers are crisp-tender.

In a large salad bowl, put lettuces, eggs and steak mixture. Pour dressing over and toss gently to coat.

SUBMARINE SALAD
*All the ingredients of a great Italian hoagie, tossed together in
a big bowl and topped with giant homemade croutons.*

Serves 6

Dressing:
    1/2 cup olive oil
    1/4 cup salad vinegar
    1 1/2 tablespoons prepared brown mustard
    2 tablespoons chopped, fresh oregano (or 1/2 teaspoon dried)
    1/2 teaspoon salt
    1/4 teaspoon pepper
    Pinch sugar

Place all ingredients in a jar with a screw-on lid, shake well, and refrigerate until serving time.

Salad:	1/2 head iceberg lettuce, coarsely chopped
	2 medium tomatoes, sliced and quartered
	2 hard-boiled eggs, sliced
	1/4 pound sliced, smoked turkey, cut into slivers
	5 - 6 slices Genoa or hard salami, cut into wedges
	6 slices provolone cheese, cut into slivers
	1/2 small onion, thinly sliced
	1/4 cup mild hot pepper rings
Croutons:	1/2 loaf fresh, unsliced Italian bread
	1 tablespoon butter or margarine
	3 tablespoons vegetable oil
	Salt to taste

In a large salad bowl, combine all salad ingredients. Pour dressing over and toss.

For croutons, cut bread into 2" cubes. In medium skillet, melt butter with oil, and fry bread cubes in a single layer until browned on all sides. Sprinkle with a little salt. Just before serving, top salad with giant croutons.

ROASTED SWEET PEPPER and ANCHOVY SALAD
Potent. You've gotta love anchovies for this one.

Serves 6

5 - 6 large, sweet bell peppers; red, yellow, green, orange,
   black or any other color they'll come up with next
1/3 cup good quality olive oil
2 tablespoons freshly squeezed lemon juice
1/2 teaspoon pepper
2 ounce tin anchovy fillets, drained

Preheat oven to broil. Place tin foil on bottom rack of oven to catch drippings. Place peppers on top rack. Broil until charred, turning occasionally. This will take 15 - 20 minutes. Put immediately in paper bag, close tightly and let rest 10 minutes. Rub skin off peppers, remove seeds and excess membrane, and cut into strips. Refrigerate in medium bowl for one hour.

In small bowl, whisk together olive oil, lemon juice and pepper. Chop anchovy fillets and stir in. Pour over chilled peppers and toss gently. Goes especially well with a good steak.

SEAGARDEN SALAD

*A pasta salad with crab, cauliflower and other
garden goodies in a creamy garlic dressing.*

Serves 4 - 6

Dressing: 3/4 cup mayonnaise
       1/4 cup milk
        2 cloves garlic, crushed
        2 tablespoons fresh dill, chopped (or 1/2 teaspoon
          dried)
        1 teaspoon lemon pepper
        1 teaspoon salt

Whisk all ingredients together in a small bowl. Set aside.

Salad: 1/2 large head cauliflower (or 1 small)
        1 cup sliced radishes
       1/4 cup sliced scallions
       1/2 pound shredded crab meat (or you can use imitation
         crab)
        3 hard-boiled eggs, chopped
        2 cups sea shell pasta; cooked, rinsed in cold water,
         and drained well

Break cauliflower in florets and place in large, glass bowl with just a little
water. Microwave 3 - 4 minutes until very crisp-tender. Drain and chill. Add
remaining ingredients, pour dressing over, and toss well. Chill again before
serving. Great with sticky buns.

MIXED GREENS with GRAPES, WALNUTS and GOAT CHEESE in HONEY-LEMON DRESSING

That long, descriptive title needs no extra gift wrap.
Your taste buds should already be standing at attention.

Serves 4 - 6

Salad:
- 1/2 cup coarsely chopped walnuts
- 1 medium head romaine lettuce
- 6 leaves red-leaf lettuce, washed and torn into bite-sized pieces
- 4 ounce log goat cheese (chevre)
- 1 cup seedless green grapes (halved if large)

Dressing:
- 1/4 cup olive oil
- Juice of 1/2 lemon
- 1 teaspoon honey

Preheat oven to 375 degrees. Spread walnut pieces on a small baking sheet and roast about 6 minutes. Set aside to cool.

Prepare romaine by discarding outer leaves (or save them for a rabbit friend). Rinse remaining leaves and break into bite-sized pieces. Mix with the red leaf lettuce, wrap in a tea towel, and refrigerate.

In a large bowl, crumble cheese. Add grapes, walnuts, and both lettuces.

In a small bowl, make dressing by whisking together all ingredients. Pour over salad and toss until coated.

BROCCOLI-TOMATO SALAD with GRAINY MUSTARD DRESSING

Tangy and colorful. Leftovers are great the next day.
If you have any, that is.

Serves 4

Dressing:
- 1/2 cup olive oil
- 1/4 cup wine vinegar
- 1/2 teaspoon salt
- 1/8 teaspoon pepper
- 2 tablespoons freshly chopped basil leaves
- 1/8 teaspoon sugar
- 3 tablespoons grainy mustard (with seeds)
- 1 clove garlic, minced

Put all ingredients in a jar with a screw-on lid and shake well. Set aside.

Salad:
- 1 1/2 pounds broccoli
- 3 medium tomatoes
- 1 tablespoon very thinly sliced shallots
- 3 hard-boiled eggs, sliced

Trim broccoli. Break into florets and cut stems into bite-sized pieces. Cook in microwave in a little water until crisp-tender, about 6 minutes. Drain and place in large glass bowl. While warm, pour dressing over and let cool.

Peel tomatoes by plunging into boiling water for 15 seconds. Coarsely chop, discarding seeds. Add tomatoes to broccoli along with shallots and eggs. Toss and chill 1 hour.

55

SAUERKRAUT POTATO SALAD with KIELBASA

*Sometimes, but not too often, there is nothing like
the taste of sauerkraut - especially in this mustard-seed
dotted potato salad. Wonderful all year 'round.*

Serves 6 - 8

Dressing:
- 3/4 cup olive oil
- 1/4 cup tarragon vinegar
- 1 teaspoon yellow mustard seeds
- 1 teaspoon caraway seeds
- 1/4 teaspoon sugar
- 1 teaspoon salt
- 1/2 teaspoon pepper

Place all ingredients in a jar with a screw-on lid. Shake well and set aside.

- 4 pounds potatoes, peeled and cut into bite-sized pieces
- 1 pound fresh sauerkraut, drained (canned is fine, too)
- 1/2 pound cooked kielbasa, sliced thin and halved

Steam or microwave potato chunks until fork tender, 8 to 12 minutes. Let cool slightly. Transfer to a large bowl and pour dressing over. Add sauerkraut and kielbasa and toss gently. Best served at room temperature.

BANANA-CHERRY-BERRY SALAD
with CREAM CHEESE DRESSING

My favorite fruits tossed in the most dreamy dressing.
Delicious for breakfast...no, lunch...no, wait, dinner -
especially in summer...no, spring....

Serves 4 - 6

Dressing: 3 ounces cream cheese, softened
1 tablespoon honey
1 tablespoon freshly squeezed lemon juice
3 tablespoons orange juice
1/4 teaspoon salt

In a food processor with a plastic blade, place all ingredients and process until smooth.

1 cup pitted Bing cherries
2 1/2 cups berries of any kind, or a mixture, such as
raspberries, blackberries, blueberries
3 ripe, but firm bananas, sliced

Place fruit in a glass bowl. Pour dressing over and toss gently. Refrigerate until chilled. An English muffin goes well with a bowl of this.

Chapter 4

MOM'S TOP TEN TERRIFIC SANDWICHES

A collection of classic sandwiches...perfected with touches only a Mom could provide.

WORLD'S GREATEST MUSHROOM-ONION BURGERS

*Sweet, caramelized onions and sautéed mushrooms mixed
right into the meat for sloppy-free eating. All you need
is a dollop of sour cream on top to be in heaven.*

Makes 5 big burgers

4 tablespoons butter or margarine
1 large onion, chopped
6 ounces mushrooms, chopped
1 1/2 pounds ground sirloin
1 1/2 teaspoons salt
1 teaspoon pepper
1 tablespoon A1 steak sauce
Vegetable oil for frying
Flour for dredging
5 big buns, toasted
Sour cream, optional

In a large, heavy skillet, melt butter and cook onions over medium-low heat until golden brown. Add mushrooms and continue cooking until mushrooms are softened. Let sit until cool enough to handle.

In a large bowl, mix together ground sirloin, salt, pepper, steak sauce, and onion mixture. Form 5 burgers.

In same large skillet, heat a thin layer of oil. Dredge burgers in flour and fry in oil until desired doneness, turning once. Slip burgers inside a lightly toasted bun and see why it's titled what it's titled.

FRESH-GRILLED TUNA SALAD on EGG ROLLS

*Occasionally, it's nice to know tuna doesn't always grow
in cans. Water chestnuts make this salad grand.*
Makes 4 sandwiches

1 pound tuna steaks, about 3/4" thick
Olive oil
Salt
6 ounce can water chestnuts, drained and chopped
1 cup mayonnaise
1/2 teaspoon grated lemon peel
1/2 teaspoon freshly ground black pepper
4 big egg rolls

Preheat oven to broil. Brush both sides of tuna steaks with a little olive oil and sprinkle lightly with salt. Place on broiler pan and broil 10 - 12 minutes, turning once, or until you can break fish apart with a fork. Let cool.

Break tuna apart in a medium bowl. Add water chestnuts, mayonnaise, lemon peel and pepper, and toss gently. Refrigerate until chilled. Pile it high on egg rolls with leaves of cool lettuce, if you like.

CORNED BEEF on POTATO PANCAKES
I guess you could think of it as an Irish Reuben.

... TALK ABOUT THE LUCK O' THE IRISH !!

Makes 4 or 5 sandwiches

Pancakes: 6 - 7 medium potatoes, peeled and grated
              1/2 cup flour
              1 egg, beaten
              1/4 cup milk
              1 1/2 teaspoons salt
              1/2 teaspoon ground white pepper

              Vegetable oil
              Mustard and horseradish, optional
              3/4 pound lean, cooked corned beef, thinly sliced

Preheat oven to 200 degrees (for keeping potato pancakes warm while you're making them). Drain liquid from potatoes and place potatoes in a large bowl. Stir in flour, egg, milk, salt and pepper. In a large skillet over medium-low heat, heat about 3 tablespoons vegetable oil. Using a serving spoon, spoon potato mixture onto surface. Press to flatten a little. Fry a few at a time until brown and crispy on both sides, turning once (this will make 8 - 10 pancakes). Add more vegetable oil as needed. Drain on paper towels and keep warm in oven until ready to assemble.

Spread a little mustard and/or horseradish on one pancake, pile with corned beef, top with another pancake, cut in half and serve.

CHOCOLATE-PEANUT BUTTER and STRAWBERRIES on WHITE BREAD

The all-American PBJ - fancy and fit for a king.

Makes 4 - 5 sandwiches

1 cup peanut butter (smooth or chunky)
4 tablespoons chocolate syrup
8 - 10 thick slices of good, white bread
1 1/2 cups sliced strawberries

In a small bowl, mix together peanut butter and chocolate. Spread generously on 4 - 5 slices of bread. Arrange sliced strawberries on chocolate-peanut butter, top with remaining bread slices, and sink teeth into.

HOW COME... WHEN YOU DROP YOUR JELLY-BREAD, ..IT ALWAYS LANDS JELLY-SIDE DOWN?

ROAST PORK with MOLASSES BUTTER on PUMPERNICKEL

Pork tenderloin roasted in soy sauce and pepper, and topped with a slightly sweetened butter. Oh my.

Makes 4 - 5 good-sized sandwiches

5 tablespoons cold sweet butter
1 teaspoon lemon juice
1 tablespoon dark molasses
Vegetable oil
1 pound whole pork tenderloin
1/3 cup soy sauce
2 tablespoons coarsely ground black pepper
1 round loaf pumpernickel bread, unsliced

Make butter: In food processor using steel blade, cream butter. Add lemon juice and molasses and mix thoroughly. Transfer to a small dish and leave at room temperature until pork is cooked.

Preheat oven to 375 degrees. Brush small roasting pan lightly with oil. Place pork in pan and pour soy sauce over. Sprinkle with pepper. Bake, uncovered 25 minutes, spooning liquid over halfway through cooking time. When pork has lost pink color, remove from oven and let stand 15 minutes before slicing.

To assemble, slice pumpernickel into 8 or 10 1/2" thick slices. Spread molasses butter on each slice and top with pork slices.

FRIED HAM and EGG SALAD on RYE

Warm, thinly sliced fried ham strips
perched on top of cool egg salad.

Makes 4 - 5 sandwiches

5 hard-boiled eggs, chopped
2 ribs celery, finely chopped
1 1/2 tablespoons canned, grated parmesan cheese
1 teaspoon prepared brown mustard
1/3 cup mayonnaise
1/8 teaspoon salt
1/8 teaspoon pepper
2 tablespoons butter or margarine
2/3 pound thinly sliced ham, cut into 1" strips
4 scallions, thinly sliced (include a little green)
1 tablespoon brown sugar
8 - 10 slices Jewish rye bread (with caraway seeds)

Make egg salad: In medium bowl, combine eggs, celery, cheese, mustard, mayonnaise, salt and pepper.

In medium skillet, melt butter. Add ham strips and fry over medium heat until lightly browned on both sides. Add scallions to pan and cook 1 minute more. Sprinkle ham mixture with brown sugar; toss until coated and sugar is melted.

Spread egg salad on rye bread, top with grilled ham, put the top on and enjoy an egg salad sandwich with a twist. Good with barbecued potato chips.

SLOPPY MOMS

If Joe only knew my secret ingredient - peanut butter!

Makes 4 - 6

1 pound ground sirloin
2 tablespoons olive oil
1 medium onion, finely chopped
1/2 green bell pepper, finely chopped (use the other half
for Leftover Meatloaf Sandwich, page 68)
1 tomato, peeled and chopped
1 teaspoon salt
1/2 teaspoon crushed red pepper flakes
2 tablespoons crunchy peanut butter
hamburger buns or pita bread

In a medium skillet, brown sirloin in oil over medium heat, breaking up with a fork. Add onion, bell pepper, tomato (to peel it, plunge it into boiling water for 15 second and skin will come off easily), salt, and red pepper flakes. Cook 10 minutes, stirring occasionally, until liquid is almost gone but mixture is still moist. Remove from heat and stir in peanut butter. You can even fill a tortilla with it for a Sloppy Mexican. Serve with giant dill pickles.

LEFTOVER MEATLOAF SANDWICH

*Everyone knows this is why meatloaf
was invented in the first place.*

Makes 6 sandwiches

1 1/4 pound ground beef round
1/4 pound ground pork
1/2 green bell pepper, finely chopped
1 small onion, finely chopped
1/2 cup oatmeal (uncooked)
1 egg
1 teaspoon salt
1/4 teaspoon pepper
1/4 teaspoon cayenne pepper
2 - 3 hard-boiled eggs
2 tablespoons tomato paste
3 - 4 slices Swiss cheese
Fresh Italian bread, unsliced

NEXT TO POT ROAST,
...IT'S MY FAVE!

Preheat oven to 375 degrees. In a large bowl, mix first 9 ingredients (stop after the cayenne pepper). Spread meat mixture evenly in a loaf pan. Form a gully lengthwise down the center and bury the hard-boiled eggs. Bake 50 minutes.

Remove from oven and spread tomato paste on top followed by cheese slices. Return to oven and bake 20 - 25 minutes more until no longer pink inside. When slightly cooled, cut off one end and taste. Consider the rest leftovers and make yourself a big sandwich. No condiments necessary.

BURNT HOTDOGS on TOAST with MOM'S MAGIC MUSTARD

Boiled wiener-eaters are not allowed in the diner.

Serves 6

Magic Mustard: 4 tablespoons prepared yellow mustard
                       1 tablespoon ketchup
                       1 tablespoon mayonnaise
                       1 tablespoon minced sweet pickle
                       1 tablespoon minced Jalepeno peppers from a jar

                       1 package of 8 good quality hotdogs
                       3 tablespoons butter or margarine
                   12 slices white bread, lightly toasted

Prepare mustard by mixing all ingredients in a small bowl.

Cut hotdogs in half widthwise. Cut each piece in half lengthwise, not cutting all the way through. Melt butter in large skillet. Cook hotdogs over medium-high heat until nicely blackened in spots, but not all over. Arrange on toast and top with Magic Mustard. Allow skillet to soak overnight.

69

BANANA SPLIT SANDWICH

A soda fountain favorite between two toasted waffles.

Gather together:

Toaster waffles
Bananas, sliced lengthwise to fit waffle
Chocolate syrup or fudge sauce
Vanilla ice cream
Chopped salted peanuts
Canned whipped cream
Chopped maraschino cherries, if you feel like it

For each Banana Split Sandwich: Toast two waffles and let cool 1 minute. Cover one with banana slices, then some chocolate syrup, then ice cream, then chopped peanuts, then more chocolate syrup, then whipped cream, then cherries. Top with a second waffle and lean over the sink when you eat it.

Chapter 5

THE BOTTOMLESS COOKIE JAR

What an awful feeling...reaching into the cookie jar, and coming up with nothing but a few crumbs. A cookie jar needs constant feeding, and just look at the goodies that follow!

BUTTERBALLS with CURRANTS

Delicate, melts in your mouth - with just the right amount of crumbliness.

Makes 40 - 45

1 cup (2 sticks) cold sweet butter, cut into chunks
1/4 cup confectioners' sugar (no need to sift)
1 teaspoon vanilla extract
2 cups flour
2/3 cup currants
More confectioners' sugar for coating

Preheat oven to 350 degrees. In food processor with plastic blade, cream butter and sugar until fluffy. Mix in vanilla. Blend in flour and fold in currants last. Dough will be crumbly.

Form dough into 1" balls by squeezing it in your hand. Place on ungreased baking sheet (you can put them close together, but not touching) and bake 18 - 20 minutes, or until very lightly golden. Let cool on baking sheet 5 minutes before transferring to wire rack.

PEANUT BUTTER SMOOCHIES

Extra easy - only 5 ingredients.

Makes 36

3 uncooked egg whites, room temperature
1/4 teaspoon cream of tartar
3/4 cup sugar
1 teaspoon vanilla extract
3/4 cup creamy peanut butter (not homemade)

Preheat oven to 300 degrees. Butter cookie sheet or line with parchment paper.

Beat together egg whites and cream of tartar with electric mixer until soft peaks form. Slowly beat in sugar until mixture is stiff. Gently fold in vanilla and peanut butter.   Drop by teaspoonfuls onto prepared baking sheet and bake 25 - 30 minutes or until very lightly browned. Cool on wire racks.

FUDGE TOOTSIES

Extra chewy and chocolatey - more like candy.

Makes 25 - 30 (easily doubled if you need more)

2 cans (14 ounce) sweetened condensed milk
6 tablespoons powdered cocoa
2 tablespoons sweet butter
2/3 cup finely chopped nuts of your choice

In a large saucepan, cook milk, cocoa and butter over low heat 20 minutes, stirring constantly with a wooden spoon. Mixture is done when you lift pan off heat, push mixture to one side and it holds its shape. Spread out on platter and allow to cool, about 30 minutes.

Meanwhile, preheat oven to 375 degrees. Spread chopped nuts on baking sheet and bake 5 minutes, or until lightly toasted. Let cool.

Take about a teaspoons worth of the cooled fudge, roll it lightly into a ball and press it in the toasted nuts. They look nice in those pretty little paper cups.

DATE-WALNUT ELEPHANT COOKIES

A giant, delicious shortbread-style cookie
that's suitable for sharing.

3/4 cup sweet butter (1 1/2 sticks)
1/2 cup sugar
1/2 teaspoon vanilla extract
1 1/3 cups flour
3/4 cup chopped walnuts
1/2 cup chopped dried dates
1/8 teaspoon salt

Preheat oven to 350 degrees. In a food processor with a steel blade, mix together butter, sugar and vanilla until crumbly. Do not overmix. Remove to a large bowl.

In another bowl, combine flour, walnuts, dates and salt. Add to the butter mixture and mix with hands. It will be very crumbly.

Press firmly and evenly into a 9" pie plate. Bake 45 minutes or until lightly browned. After cooling, remove from pie plate and break off a big chunk.

For frosting: In a food processor with steel blade, cream together butter, cream cheese and orange juice concentrate. Add confectioners' sugar and mix until creamy. Frost cooled brownies and cut into squares. You can also grate more orange peel over the top.

COFFEE BEAN-SUGAR COOKIES
Big, plump sugar cookies punctuated with crunchy, bitter coffee beans.

Makes 30 big cookies

3/4 cup coffee beans (your favorite flavor)
1 cup (2 sticks) sweet butter, softened
1 cup sugar (plus more for rolling)
2 egg yolks
1 teaspoon vanilla extract
2 1/2 cups flour
1/2 teaspoon baking soda
1/2 teaspoon salt

Preheat oven to 350 degrees. Spread coffee beans on baking sheet and bake 10 minutes, shaking occasionally. Let cool.

In food processor with steel blade, cream butter and sugar. Blend in egg yolks and vanilla. In another bowl, combine flour, baking soda and salt. Add to butter mixture and mix in. Fold in coffee beans (dough will be dry).

Roll into large 1 1/2" balls. Roll each ball in sugar. Place 2" apart on ungreased baking sheet and slightly flatten with the bottom of a glass. Bake 12 - 15 minutes until bottoms are light brown (cookies will be puffy). Let cool 1 minute on pan before removing to wire rack. Good with a tall glass of cold milk.

SORTA LIKE OREOS ONLY DIFFERENT
Chewy, brownie-like sandwich cookies.

Makes 40

Cookies:
- 6 squares (1 ounce each) semi-sweet chocolate
- 3 squares (1 ounce each) unsweetened chocolate
- 2 tablespoons butter or margarine
- 2 eggs
- 1 cup sugar
- 1/3 cup flour
- 1/2 teaspoon baking powder
- 1 teaspoon salt
- 1/2 teaspoon vanilla extract

Filling:
- 1 1/2 tablespoons sweet butter, melted
- 2 tablespoons + 1 teaspoon light cream or half and half
- 2 cups sifted confectioners' sugar

For cookies: Preheat oven to 350 degrees. Butter baking sheet or line with parchment paper.

In top of a double boiler over hot, not boiling water, melt both chocolates with butter. Let cool.

In medium bowl, beat eggs with sugar. Combine flour, baking powder and salt and add to egg mixture. Stir in vanilla and melted chocolate mixture. Let batter stand 5 minutes to stiffen. Drop by half teaspoonfuls 2" apart on prepared baking sheet and bake 8 - 10 minutes or just until set (cookies will be soft, but they'll firm up after cooling).

For filling: In a small bowl, combine butter and cream. Add confectioners' sugar 1/3 at a time, blending with a fork. Let cookies completely cool before filling.

There are two ways you can eat these. You can plunge them into your mouth all at once, followed by a swig of milk; or you can twist the top off, lick the cream filling off, and dip them in milk until soft.

Chapter 6

EAT YOUR VEGETABLES
AND YOU'LL GROW BIG AND TALL

No child was ever raised without hearing
"EAT YOUR VEGETABLES!" a thousand times at least.
A good vegetable dish can sometimes outshine
the main course. Here's proof.

POOR MAN'S CAVIAR
Roasted eggplant dip with plenty of onions and garlic.

Makes 1 1/2 cups

1 large eggplant (1 1/2 - 2 pounds)
2 cloves garlic, minced
3 tablespoons freshly squeezed lemon juice
1/2 cup chopped Spanish onion
1 tablespoon chopped fresh parsley
1/2 teaspoon salt
1/4 teaspoon pepper
Cocktail rye bread or crackers

Preheat oven to broil. Place eggplant on foil-lined baking sheet. Broil, turning once or twice, until skin is charred all over and eggplant has collapsed (I know how it feels sometimes). This can take 20 - 30 minutes. Remove and let cool. Remove stem and peel skin off.

In a food processor with a steel blade, combine eggplant pulp (seeds and all) with remaining ingredients and blend until smooth. Serve with cocktail rye or crackers at room temperature for best flavor.

Note: If you want a milder onion flavor, cook chopped onion in 1 - 2 tablespoons of olive oil until soft.

CREAMED CORN ON THE COB

*Corn on the cob is great just plain. Just imagine
it extra creamy and buttery. Heaven on earth.*

For 12 ears

12 ears fresh picked corn on the cob
6 tablespoons butter, softened
5 tablespoons heavy cream
1 tablespoon salt
1/2 teaspoon freshly ground black pepper

Preheat oven to 400 degrees. Place metal steamer basket in the bottom of a large pot and add water to the bottom of the basket. Stand corn in, bring to a boil, cover, and steam 6 minutes. Remove to a roasting pan and let cool.

In a medium bowl, beat butter and cream together with a fork. Stir in salt and pepper. Brush half the butter mixture on the corn and bake 4 - 5 minutes (you can also cook them on the grill over medium heat). Remove from oven or grill and brush corn with remaining butter mixture. I could have this as the main course.

PAN-COOKED GREEN BEANS in MUSTARD
Tangy, garlicky and ever so easy.

Serves 4 - 6

1 pound green beans, ends trimmed
2 tablespoons sweet butter
1 clove garlic, minced
1 tablespoon + 1 teaspoon grainy brown mustard
Freshly ground black pepper to taste

Place beans in a glass bowl with 3 tablespoons water and microwave on high 4 minutes, uncovered. Drain.

In large skillet, melt butter over medium-low heat. As it is melting, add garlic. Stir in mustard. Add beans and toss to coat. Cook 2 - 3 minutes. Season with pepper and serve.

WAX BEANS in ORANGE BUTTER
Crisp-tender beans, lightly bathed in orange.

Serves 4 - 6

1 pound fresh wax beans (the yellow ones)
2 tablespoons butter or margarine
2 teaspoons orange juice concentrate

Microwave beans in 2 tablespoons water 5 minutes. Drain. In medium skillet, melt butter, stir in orange juice, add beans and heat through. Period.

STEAMED BROCCOLI with CHOPPED-EGG SAUCE

Made better with a little sharp Cheddar.

Serves 6

2 pounds fresh broccoli
3 tablespoons butter or margarine
1/4 cup flour
1 1/4 cups hot milk
1/2 teaspoon salt
1/4 teaspoon pepper
3 hard-boiled eggs, chopped
1/2 cup shredded sharp Cheddar cheese

Trim broccoli. Break into florets and cut stem into bite-sized pieces. Place in a large, glass bowl with 3 tablespoons water. Microwave on high 8 - 10 minutes or until fork-tender.

Meanwhile, make sauce: melt butter in a medium saucepan over medium-low heat. Stir in flour and cook 1 minute. Gradually add milk, stirring constantly. Season with salt and pepper. Simmer about 5 minutes, or until it thickens. Stir in eggs and cheese. Drain broccoli and pour sauce over.

SPINACH PUDDING

So wonderfully puffy and tasty, you'd hardly know it
was a vegetable. Even brings raves from children.

Serves 6

6 tablespoons butter or margarine
1/2 pound fresh spinach, rinsed well in cold water, stems
removed, chopped
1/4 teaspoon ground nutmeg
3/4 teaspoon salt
1/8 teaspoon pepper
1/4 cup grated Parmesan cheese from a can
1 1/2 cups milk
4 eggs, beaten
1 cup fresh, white bread crumbs (about 2 slices,
processed in food processor with steel blade)

Preheat oven to 350 degrees. Butter an 8" round casserole dish.

In large saucepan, melt butter. Add spinach and cook over medium heat until wilted, about 5 minutes. Remove saucepan from heat. Stir in all remaining ingredients.

Pour into prepared casserole and bake 55 - 60 minutes, or until golden on top and set.

COCONUT CAULIFLOWER
Whole, steamed cauliflower doused with a touch of the tropics.

Serves 6

1 large, whole cauliflower, trimmed
2 tablespoons vegetable oil
1 medium onion, chopped
2/3 cup sweetened flake coconut
2 tablespoons freshly squeezed lemon juice
1/8 teaspoon cayenne pepper
1/4 teaspoon salt
5 tablespoons milk

Place metal steamer basket in large pot with lid. Add enough water to reach holes. Put in cauliflower, bring to boil, cover, and steam over medium heat 15 minutes or until fork tender.

Meanwhile, heat vegetable oil in medium saucepan. Add onion and cook until softened, about 5 minutes. Add coconut and cook, stirring, until coconut is light brown. Transfer to food processor with steel blade and add lemon juice, cayenne pepper and salt and process several minutes, scraping sides until mixture is of fine consistency. Add milk and mix. Transfer mixture back to saucepan and heat through on very low heat.

Place cooked cauliflower in bowl, spoon coconut sauce over, and serve.

LOOK, THIS RELATIONSHIP IS JUST AS NEW FOR ME AS IT IS FOR YOU... SO RELAX AND ENJOY IT !!

TWICE-BAKED SWEET POTATOES with MARSHMALLOWS

The marshmallows melt right into the potato and produce the tastiest, most nostalgic flavor. Like Thanksgiving all year 'round.

OH, THANK YOU, THANK YOU, THANK YOU...

Serves 6

3 large sweet potatoes
3 tablespoons sweet butter, softened
3 tablespoons light cream or half and half
1/4 teaspoon salt
1/2 cup miniature marshmallows
2 tablespoons brown sugar

Preheat oven to 375 degrees. Wash each potato and pierce several times with a fork. Place directly on top oven rack. Bake 1 hour 10 minutes, or until tender. Let cool enough to handle. Keep oven on.

Slice potatoes in half lengthwise and scoop out pulp into a large bowl, leaving enough for a sturdy shell. Add butter, cream and salt and beat with an electric mixer until smooth. By hand, fold in marshmallows. Stuff skins with mixture.

Lightly oil roasting pan with vegetable oil. Place stuffed potatoes in pan, sprinkle each top with 1 teaspoon brown sugar, and return to oven. Bake 15 minutes more, or until heated through. Give thanks.

BAKED GINGER ONIONS

What a wonderful aroma while these are baking!

Serves 6

6 medium - large yellow onions
6 tablespoons butter or margarine
1 tablespoon ground ginger
1 teaspoon salt
1/2 cup beef stock or broth

Preheat oven to 375 degrees. Peel onions and cut in half widthwise. Melt butter in 8" x 8" square pan in hot oven. Stir in ginger and salt. Place onions, cut side down, in pan and spoon seasoned butter over. Bake, uncovered, 30 minutes. Pour beef stock over and bake 20 minutes more, or until onions are very tender.

BROWN SUGAR SPUDS

*Not too sweet, but just different enough to
surpass boiled potatoes in a contest.*

Serves 8

10 medium Idaho potatoes, peeled and cut into 2" chunks
6 tablespoons sweet butter, melted
2 tablespoons brown sugar
1/2 teaspoon cayenne pepper
pinch salt

Place potato chunks in bowl with 3 tablespoons water. Microwave 6 - 8 minutes, or until fork tender. Drain.

Preheat oven to broil. In a small bowl, mix butter, brown sugar, cayenne, and salt. Place potato chunks in a roasting pan and pour butter mixture over. Broil 6 - 8 minutes, or until potatoes are browned and glazed.

APPLE SMASHED POTATOES
Creamy, cinnamony casserole-style potatoes.

Serves 6

4 large potatoes, peeled and cut into chunks
1/4 cup (1/2 stick) butter or margarine, softened
2 tablespoons heavy cream
2 tablespoons sugar
1/2 teaspoon cinnamon
1 egg
1 1/2 cups unsweetened applesauce

Preheat oven to 375 degrees. Butter an 8" round casserole dish.

In a large saucepan, boil potato chunks until tender, about 15 minutes. Quickly drain in colander and return to saucepan. Add butter and cream and beat with electric mixer until smooth. Add sugar, cinnamon, egg and applesauce and mix well.

Turn into prepared casserole dish and bake 25 minutes, uncovered, or until top is lightly browned.

FARMERS MARKET PIZZA

A harvest of healthy vegetables hidden beneath
a layer of cheese in a slightly sweetened crust.

Serves 6 (2 slices each)

Dough:
- 1/2 cup warm water
- 1 packet dry yeast
- 1 teaspoon sugar
- 1/2 teaspoon salt
- 1 tablespoon olive oil
- 1 3/4 cups fine flour (like Wondra)
- 2 tablespoons melted butter

Topping:
- 1/2 cup tomato sauce
- 1 1/2 cups *each* broccoli and cauliflower florets, microwaved until crisp tender (5 minutes)
- 1/2 red bell pepper, cut into strips
- 1/2 cup sliced zucchini
- 1/2 small onion, chopped
- 1 can (14 ounces) artichoke hearts, drained and coarsely chopped
- 1/2 cup freshly grated Parmesan cheese
- 2 1/2 cups freshly grated mozzarella cheese

Make crust: Preheat oven to 375 degrees. Pour water into a medium bowl, add yeast and stir until dissolved. Pour into food processor bowl with steel blade. Add sugar, salt, olive oil and 1 cup flour and blend until smooth. Add remaining flour and beat until dough is stiff.

Place dough on a floured surface and knead until soft and pliable. Put in lightly oiled bowl, brush with a little olive oil, cover with a damp towel, and place in warm spot for 1 hour, or until dough doubles in size.

Punch dough down and, using a rolling pin, roll into a circle (or rectangle) about 1/8" thick to fit baking/pizza pan. Grease pan with melted butter and place dough on it. Or, if you're in a hurry, buy an already-made-ready-to-top-crust.

For topping, spread tomato sauce over dough and arrange all vegetables on top. Sprinkle with Parmesan cheese, then cover generously with mozzarella. Bake 25 minutes or until crust is brown and cheese is bubbly.

DEEP-FRIED ARTICHOKE BOTTOMS
with LEMON MAYONNAISE
The best part of an artichoke - fried
crispy and tender with the perfect dip.

Serves 6 - 8

2 cans (14 ounces each) artichoke bottoms
4 eggs, beaten
1/2 cup flour
1 cup fine dry Italian-style bread crumbs
3 tablespoons grated Parmesan cheese (canned)
canola oil for frying
1/2 cup mayonnaise
2 - 3 tablespoons freshly squeezed lemon juice

Rinse and drain artichoke bottoms. Cut into quarters, or bite-sized pieces. Pat dry with paper towels. Get 3 shallow bowls. Put eggs in one, flour in another, and bread crumbs mixed with cheese in the last.

Heat 1 1/2" oil in large, deep skillet. Dip artichoke pieces in egg, then flour, then egg again, and finally coat with bread crumb mixture. Fry in batches until golden brown. Drain on paper towels.

In a small bowl, mix mayonnaise with lemon juice and dip warm artichoke bottoms in. A great main course accompaniment that can also be served as an appetizer.

Chapter 7

THE BLUES PLATE SPECIAL

Mouth-watering Mashed Potato-Meatloaf Pie, tart Fried Green Tomatoes, puffy Poppyseed Popovers, stick-to-your-fork Chocolate Malt Devil's Food Cake... all that's needed is some good jazz to complete the meal.

POPPYSEED POPOVERS

I just love breaking open these big, hollow rolls.
The flavor is rich and eggy and needs just
a touch of sweet butter before indulging.

Makes 4 (easily doubled)

2/3 cup flour
1/4 teaspoon salt
1/3 cup milk
1/3 cup water
2 eggs
1/4 cup shredded Cheddar cheese
1 1/2 teaspoons poppy seeds
4 tablespoons butter or margarine

Preheat oven to 375 degrees. In medium bowl, combine flour and salt. Add milk and water and mix until smooth. Beat in eggs. Fold in cheese and poppy seeds.

Place 1 tablespoon butter in each of 4 large (8 ounce) oven-proof custard cups. Put cups on baking sheet and put in oven for 4 - 5 minutes until butter melts. Remove from oven and with a pastry brush, coat the inside of the cups with the butter.

Fill cups half full with batter and bake 45 - 50 minutes without peeking until towards the end. They should be a deep golden brown (if they're not done enough, they'll deflate).

MASHED POTATO-MEATLOAF PIE

Two of the most delicious comfort foods
ever invented, together in one handsome pie.

Serves 4 - 6

Meatloaf filling:
- 2 tablespoons butter or margarine
- 1 tablespoon vegetable oil
- 1 small green bell pepper, chopped
- 1 small onion, thinly sliced
- 3/4 pound ground beef chuck
- 1 egg
- 1/4 cup ketchup
- 1/2 cup dry bread crumbs
- 1/2 teaspoon salt
- 1/2 teaspoon pepper
- 1/2 teaspoon cayenne pepper
- 2 tablespoons light cream or half and half

- 1 deep dish unbaked pie shell (9")

Potato topping:
- 2 large potatoes, peeled and cut into large chunks
- 2 tablespoons sweet butter
- 1/2 teaspoon salt
- 1/4 teaspoon pepper
- 1 tablespoon light cream
- 1/2 cup shredded Cheddar cheese

Preheat oven to 375 degrees.

For meat filling: in a small skillet, heat butter with oil. Cook bell pepper and onion until onion is golden. Transfer to a large bowl. Add the remaining meat filling ingredients and mix thoroughly with hands. Spread mixture in pie shell and bake 30 minutes.

Make potato topping: while meat is cooking, boil or steam potatoes until tender, about 15 minutes. Drain and return to saucepan or dish. Add butter, salt, pepper and cream and beat with an electric mixer until smooth and fluffy. Fold in cheese.

Remove meat pie from oven and mound potato mixture on top. Return to oven and bake 20 minutes more. Turn oven to broil and lightly brown the top to give it a nice look.

Note: This recipe may look tedious because of the long ingredient list, but you'll already have most of the things on hand - and it's really quite simple to make.

FRIED GREEN TOMATOES in CREAM

*I have to admit - I stole this recipe..but I politely asked
to steal this recipe, and Bonnie said yes. There is just
no better way to enjoy fried green tomatoes than this.*

Serves 4

4 good-sized green tomatoes, unpeeled
Flour for dredging (seasoned with a little salt and pepper)
3 tablespoons sweet butter
1 tablespoon brown sugar
1/2 cup heavy cream

Trim ends off tomatoes and discard. Slice tomatoes 1/2" thick. Dredge in
seasoned flour.

In a large, heavy skillet, melt butter over medium heat. When it begins to
sizzle, add tomato slices in single layer. Sprinkle with brown sugar, using
1 1/2 teaspoons. When lightly browned, turn and sprinkle with remaining
brown sugar. When tomatoes are browned and starting to soften, turn off
the heat and immediately pour in cream. Turn tomatoes gently to coat, and
as far as I'm concerned, stand there and eat them right out of the pan.

Chapter 8

A HOMEMADE TV DINNER

Remember those Friday nights...the T.V. tables snapped into place...the sectioned aluminum trays with Salisbury steak, instant mashed potatoes, mixed vegies, and Apple Crisp? Well, now try my homemade version. Great for when company comes.

SALISBURY STEAK SURPRISE
with GROUND MUSHROOM GRAVY

I'll give you a hint - the surprise is blue and it has to do with cheese. One of my most delectable dishes.

Serves 4

2 pounds ground beef sirloin
3 tablespoons finely chopped onion
2 tablespoons tomato paste
1 teaspoon salt
1/2 teaspoon pepper
1 block (4 ounces) blue cheese, quartered
2 tablespoons vegetable oil
3 tablespoons butter or margarine
Flour for dredging
1 cup beef stock or broth
1/2 pound mushrooms, trimmed

In large bowl, mix together ground sirloin, onion, tomato paste, salt and pepper. Form into 4 oval patties. Bury a piece of blue cheese in the center of each patty, sealing well (squish cheese together a little).

Melt oil and butter in a large, heavy skillet. Dredge patties in flour and, over medium heat, brown on both sides. Pour beef stock over, cover, and cook 20 minutes. Remove steaks to a platter and keep warm.

Put mushrooms in food processor with steel blade. Process until finely ground. Add to steak pan and simmer 10 minutes, or until thickened.

NUTMEG MASHED POTATOES

Perfect with my Salisbury steak, and
it gives the gravy a good place to rest.

Serves 4

4 large Idaho potatoes, peeled and cut into big chunks
4 tablespoons sweet butter, softened
3 tablespoons light cream or half and half
1/2 teaspoon ground nutmeg
1 teaspoon salt
1/4 teaspoon ground white pepper

Boil potatoes until fork-tender, 15 - 20 minutes. Drain and immediately add remaining ingredients to potatoes. Beat with electric mixer until smooth and creamy. Heat through over very low heat, stirring.

MIXED VEGETABLE HASH

A bevy of colorful vegetables, grated
and cooked in a skillet just like hash browns.

Serves 4

1 large potato, peeled
2 large carrots, trimmed and scraped
2 medium zucchini (about 2/3 pound)
1 medium onion, peeled
3 tablespoons butter or margarine
3 tablespoons vegetable oil

In food processor using shredding blade, shred potato, carrots, zucchini and onion. Remove blade and mix with hands.

Heat butter and oil in large skillet. Spread vegetables evenly over bottom and cook over medium heat about 5 minutes without touching. When starting to brown, pie-cut into four wedges and carefully turn with a large metal spatula. Continue cooking another 4 or 5 minutes until second side is lightly browned. Season with salt and pepper, if you wish.

SOUR CHERRY-BANANA-CHOCOLATE CHIP CRISP

The crisp, of course, is the best part -
and there's plenty of it in this lucious recipe.

Serves 9

2 cans (16 ounces each) pitted tart cherries in water
1 cup sugar, divided
1/3 cup cornstarch
1/8 teaspoon salt
1/2 teaspoon vanilla extract
2 bananas, sliced into rounds
1/2 cup firmly packed brown sugar
3/4 cup flour
1/2 cup (1 stick) cold sweet butter, cut into chunks
3/4 cup quick-cooking (not instant) oats
3/4 cup semi-sweet chocolate chips
Vanilla bean ice cream

Preheat oven to 375 degrees. Drain cherries, reserving 1 cup juice.

In a large saucepan, combine 3/4 cup of the sugar, cornstarch and salt. Slowly whisk in reserved juice. Cook over medium-low heat, stirring constantly, until thickened. Remove from heat and stir in cherries, vanilla extract, bananas and remaining 1/4 cup sugar. Spoon into a 9" x 9" square pan.

In a medium bowl, combine brown sugar, flour and oatmeal. With fingers, work butter in until it resembles coarse meal. Stir in chocolate chips. Sprinkle over cherry mixture.

Bake 40 minutes or until top is golden brown. Serve warm (not hot) with a scoop of vanilla bean ice cream.

Note: This can be assembled ahead of time up to the baking point and refrigerated until later. Don't make it too much later, though, because bananas can turn kind of funny after awhile.

Another note: Use one 2-cup measuring cup to measure all the ingredients and save on dishes.

Chapter 9

CHUCK WAGON CHOW

Inspired by the colorful cowboys of the old west
... sitting around a campfire, drinking coffee
from a tin cup and enjoying the rib-sticking
fare served from the back of a chuck wagon.
——— GET YOUR EATIN IRONS READY !

SWEET and SOUR COWCUMBERS

*Cowcumbers meant pickles and this crunchy version
can be eaten 'longside just about any meal.*

Makes a whole lot

1 great big jar of whole dill pickles
2 cups sugar
1 cup cider vinegar
1 cinnamon stick
1 teaspoon celery seeds
1 teaspoon yellow mustard seeds
1 teaspoon whole cloves

Drain and rinse pickles. Cut into bite-sized chunks.

In a medium saucepan, put sugar, vinegar and cinnamon stick. Bring to a boil, reduce heat, and simmer 15 minutes. Remove cinnamon stick and discard. Add remaining spices, remove from heat, and cool.

Return cowcumber chunks to jar, pour syrup over and store in refrigerator.

COWCUMBERS ?
...I'M CONFUSED!!

BAKED WHISTLE BERRIES in BEER

*(Baked beans to a cowboy). A casserole of Great Northern Beans
in a dandy, not-too-sweet sauce that's perfect with ribs.*

Serves 6 - 8

4 slices thin-cut bacon
1 medium onion, finely chopped
2 cloves garlic, minced
3 cans (14 ounces each) Great Northern Beans, drained
1/2 cup molasses
3 tablespoons brown sugar
2/3 cup beer
3 tablespoons prepared brown mustard
1/4 teaspoon bottled cayenne pepper sauce

Preheat oven to 350 degrees. In a small skillet, fry bacon until crisp. Drain on paper towels. Add onion and garlic to bacon fat in skillet and cook until softened.

Put beans in a large casserole dish. Add cooked onion mixture, molasses, brown sugar, beer, mustard and pepper sauce. mix well. Crumble bacon over the top.

Cover and bake 30 minutes. Uncover and bake 30 minutes more, or until beans have a nice sauce without being too soupy. Serve warm.

TOMBSTONE BONES

Mighty tasty salt 'n vinegar ribs.
So easy to make, it's like ropin' a two-legged calf.

Serves 4

4 pounds pork spareribs
3/4 cup apple cider vinegar
1 1/2 teaspoons salt
1 teaspoon pepper
1 1/4 teaspoons sugar

Preheat campfire to 375 degrees. Place ribs in roasting pan. Add 2 cups water, cover tightly with heavy foil and bake 45 minutes.

Meanwhile (back at the ranch), combine vinegar, salt, pepper and sugar in a small bowl.

Remove ribs from oven and drain water. Raise oven temperature to 500 degrees. Pour vinegar sauce over ribs, return to oven, and bake, uncovered 25 minutes more, basting once or twice. Finger food, sure as shootin'.

Note: You can also cook these on the grill after the oven steaming part. Just baste with sauce while they're grilling.

DEATH VALLEY CHILI

*Black beans and ground turkey in a chicken broth
so packed with pepper your mouth'll feel like a smokin' pistol.*

Serves 8 - 10

1 pound dried black beans (you can cheat and use the
    canned kind if you want - 2 pounds worth, drained)
2 medium onions, coarsely chopped
4 tablespoons butter or margarine
1 1/2 pounds lean ground turkey
2 tablespoons flour
6 cups chicken stock or broth
2 tablespoons finely chopped fresh jalepeno peppers
1 teaspoon black pepper
1 teaspoon cayenne pepper
1 teaspoon white pepper
2 teaspoons salt
1/2 teaspoon sugar
Grated sharp Cheddar cheese

Soak and cook beans according to package directions in a large pot. Drain,
return beans to pot.

In a large skillet, melt butter. Add onions and cook until light brown. Add
turkey and cook over medium heat until pink color is gone, breaking up with
a fork. Sprinkle flour over mixture and cook 2 more minutes.

Add turkey mixture to the bean pot along with the rest of the ingredients except for the cheese. Bring to a boil, then simmer over low heat about 20 minutes, stirring occasionally. Serve with cheese sprinkled on top. It also wouldn't hurt to have a cold one near by to wash it down with.

Note: If you want it a little thicker, dissolve 2 tablespoons cornstarch in 3 tablespoons cold water, stir it in, and simmer a few more minutes.

DODGE CITY RIBS
Tender, meaty ribs drenched in a tangy, tomato-peach barbecue sauce with a nip of whiskey and a touch of pepper.

Serves 6

5 pounds western-style pork ribs (the meaty kind)
1 tablespoon freshly ground black pepper

Sauce:
28 ounce can tomato puree
1/2 cup cider vinegar
1/2 cup peach preserves
1/2 cup whiskey
1/3 cup prepared brown mustard
3 tablespoons lemon juice
1/4 cup firmly packed brown sugar
1 teaspoon salt
1/2 teaspoon ground white pepper
1/2 teaspoon crushed red pepper
3 tablespoons sweet butter

Preheat oven to 375 degrees. Place ribs in a large roasting pan with 2 cups water. Sprinkle pepper over, cover tightly with heavy foil and bake 1 hour.

Make barbecue sauce: Put all sauce ingredients in a large saucepan. Slowly bring to a boil and simmer, uncovered, 15 - 20 minutes.

Remove ribs from oven and drain water off. Increase oven temperature to 475 degrees. Pour 2 cups barbecue sauce over ribs, return to oven, and bake, uncovered, 45 more minutes. Brush with additional sauce before serving. Save any leftover sauce for the next time you'll be grilling cacklers.

Note: Ribs may also be grilled. After the 1 hour baking process, finish cooking on grill, basting frequently with sauce.

GRILLED POOCH BREAD with SKUNK EGGS

Pooch was a cowboy dish made with tomatoes, sugar and bread. Skunk eggs, were, of course, onions. This version of pooch uses sour dough bread as a base for sweetened, grilled onions and slices of tomatoes. Good with peppery dishes.

Serves 6 - 8

8 tablespoons butter or margarine
3 medium onions, sliced thin
4 tablespoons brown sugar, divided
1 loaf sour dough bread, halved lengthwise
2 medium-large tomatoes, cut into 1/4" slices

Preheat oven to 475 degrees. In a medium skillet, melt butter and cook onions over medium heat until golden. Add 2 tablespoons of the brown sugar and cook 2 minutes more, stirring.

Place bread on baking sheet, cut side up. Spoon onions on top of bread and pour butter from pan over. Top with tomato slices. Sprinkle with remaining 2 tablespoons brown sugar. Bake 10 minutes.

Turn oven to broil and cook pooch bread 2 - 3 more minutes or until tomatoes are lightly browned.

ARBUCKLE CUSTARD PIE

Arbuckle was such a popular brand of coffee in the Old West, that a cup of coffee was simply called Arbuckle. This creamy, coffee custard pie is the perfect ending to a campfire meal from the chuck wagon.

Serves 8 - 10

3 eggs
1 1/2 cups milk
1/2 cup light cream or half and half
1 teaspoon vanilla extract
1/2 cup sugar
3 tablespoons instant coffee dissolved in 1 tablespoon
warm water
9" deep dish pie crust, unbaked

Preheat oven to 400 degrees. Beat eggs in a large bowl with a wire whisk. Add remaining ingredients (except for the crust), and mix well. Place pie crust in oven rack and pour coffee custard mixture into. Bake 40 minutes.

Lower oven temperature to 300 degrees. Bake 30 minutes more, or just until set. If you must, top it with whipped cream.

GONE FISHIN'

FISH STORIES

I've hooked some real treasures for you to sink your teeth into (the only hard part was wrestling the shark.)

SWEET POTATO CRAB CAKES
Without a doubt, the best crab cakes you'll ever eat.

Makes 10 (figure 2 per person)

1 pound cooked crab meat (fresh or thawed frozen is best)
2 cups cooked, mashed sweet potatoes (that's about 2,
    pierced with a fork and microwaved on high 10 - 12
    minutes, peeled, and mashed with a fork)
3 tablespoons minced onion
2 tablespoons melted butter
1 teaspoon bottled cayenne pepper sauce
1 teaspoon salt
3 egg yolks beaten with 1/4 cup milk
3 cups fresh, white bread crumbs (about 6 slices,
    processed in a food processor, crusts and all)
1/2 cup vegetable oil
3 tablespoons butter

In a large bowl, gently mix crab, sweet potatoes, onion, butter, pepper sauce and salt. Form into 10 patties. Dip patties in egg yolk mixture and then in bread crumbs. Chill 1 hour.

In a large skillet, heat oil and butter. Fry crab cakes, a few at a time, until golden, turning once.

You can serve them with a dollop of lemon mayonnaise by mixing 2/3 cup mayonnaise with the juice of 1/2 lemon.

CORN-FLAKE SCALLOPS over GARLIC NOODLES
Baked bay scallops in a crunchy coating atop a sea
of tender noodles with plenty of garlic and fresh parsley.

Serves 4

1 pound bay scallops (the small ones)
1 cup crushed corn flakes
Butter
8 ounces medium-wide noodles, cooked according to
    package directions, and drained without rinsing
1/4 cup olive oil (extra virgin is best)
3 cloves garlic, minced
1 1/2 teaspoons salt
1/2 teaspoon pepper
3 tablespoons chopped, fresh parsley

Preheat oven to 425 degrees.

Wash scallops and dry on a tea towel (paper towels will stick). Put corn flake crumbs in a clean paper bag along with scallops and shake bag until scallops are coated. Lightly butter a baking sheet, and arrange scallops on it without touching each other. Bake 5 minutes, shake the baking sheet to loosen the scallops and bake 4 minutes more, or until crust is golden.

In a large, deep skillet, heat oil and cook garlic until lightly browned. Reduce heat to low, add noodles, salt, pepper and parsley and toss to coat noodles. Divide among plates and sprinkle scallops on top.

PAN-FRIED BUTTERMILK CATFISH

*Marinated catfish fillets, dipped in a cornmeal coating
and fried in peanut oil until golden. Good with tartar sauce.*

Serves 6

   1 egg
2/3 cup fresh buttermilk
1/2 teaspoon freshly ground black pepper
1/8 teaspoon cayenne pepper
1/2 teaspoon salt
   6 catfish fillets (about 1 1/2 pounds)
1/2 cup fine white cornmeal
1/2 cup dry, seasoned bread crumbs
   Peanut oil for frying

In a medium bowl, mix together egg, buttermilk, both peppers and salt.

Place catfish in a rectangular glass pan and pour buttermilk mixture over. Cover and refrigerate a couple of hours.

Combine cornmeal and bread crumbs in a shallow bowl and coat marinated catfish fillets.

Heat about 1/2" peanut oil in large, deep skillet (wrought iron is what I like to use). Fry fillets until nicely browned, turning once. Drain on paper towels.

LEMON-GRILLED SWORDFISH with TOMATO BUTTER
Thick, tender swordfish steaks crowned with
a generous pat of tangy, melting tomato butter.

Serves 4

Tomato butter: 1/2 cup (1 stick) sweet butter
2 tablespoons tomato paste
1 clove garlic, minced
1 tablespoon finely chopped fresh basil leaves (or 1/2
    teaspoon dried)
2 teaspoons lemon juice

4 medium (or 2 large) swordfish steaks, 1" thick
Olive oil
1 lemon, sliced thin
Sugar for dredging

Make tomato butter: In a food processor using plastic or metal blade, cream butter. Add tomato paste, garlic, basil and lemon juice and blend well. Remove blade from processor, and with hands, scoop up butter mixture and form a log shape. Wrap in plastic and refrigerate at least 1 hour.

Position top rack in oven about 6" from the top. Preheat oven to broil. Brush swordfish steaks with a little olive oil and place in roasting pan. Lightly dredge lemon slices in sugar and arrange on top of fish. Broil 15 minutes or until fork tender. Remove blackened lemon slices and discard.

Immediately place 1 or 2 slices of tomato butter on top of each swordfish steak before serving.

SALMON PAPRIKASH

*Fresh salmon steaks buried in a paprika-sour cream
sauce dotted with scallions and green pepper.*

Serves 4

1 tablespoon olive oil
3 scallions, thinly sliced (include some green)
1/2 large green bell pepper, finely chopped
2 tablespoons Hungarian paprika (medium-hot is good)
1 teaspoon salt
1/4 teaspoon pepper
16 ounces sour cream
4 salmon steaks, 1 1/4" thick
Juice of 1/2 lemon

Preheat oven to 400 degrees. Brush a broiler pan or roasting pan with oil.

In a small saucepan, heat the oil and cook scallions and green pepper over medium heat just until softened. Add paprika and stir 1 minute. Remove pan from heat and stir in salt, pepper and sour cream.

Place salmon steaks in prepared pan. Spread sauce over and squeeze lemon juice on the tops. Bake about 20 minutes, or until salmon is cooked and sauce is bubbling. Serve with a nice, green salad.

BACON-BAKED RAINBOW TROUT
Three ingredients - a million raves.

Serves 4

6 - 8 thin slices bacon
4 whole rainbow trout, heads removed and cleaned
2 tablespoons lemon pepper

Preheat oven to 400 degrees. Line a roasting pan with the bacon slices and bake 10 - 12 minutes, or until just starting to brown. Lay trout on top of bacon in single layer and sprinkle with lemon pepper. Bake, uncovered, 20 minutes. Serve with bacon alongside.

BLACKENED SHARK BITES with a CREAMY TOMATO CHASER
The first bite is almost too hot - but keep going, you will soon be addicted. The sweet and sour tomato chaser comes in real handy.

Serves 4

Seasoning mix: 1 tablespoon cayenne pepper
1 teaspoon ground white pepper
1 teaspoon black pepper
1 teaspoon garlic powder
1 teaspoon sweet paprika
1 1/2 teaspoons salt
1 teaspoon dry mustard

1/2 cup (1 stick) sweet butter, melted
1 1/2 pounds shark steaks, 1" thick, cut into 1 1/2" pieces

Tomato chaser: 1 medium tomato, peeled, seeded and coarsely chopped
1/2 cup sour cream
1 tablespoon brown sugar
2 tablespoons lemon juice

In a small bowl, mix the 7 ingredients of the seasoning mix.

Heat a large, black wrought iron skillet until it passes the sizzling water test, about 6 - 8 minutes. In the melted butter, coat the shark pieces. Then roll lightly in the seasoning mix. Fry over medium-high heat until coating is blackened and shark is tender, turning once.

Make tomato chaser by putting tomatoes in a food processor with a steel blade and whirling until pureed. Blend in sour cream, brown sugar and lemon juice. Serve it in a little cup next to the shark bites.

A FINE KETTLE OF FISH STEW

Chunks of fresh turbot simmered in a fragrant
stock that's loaded with potatoes and tomatoes.

Serves 6 - 8

6 tablespoons butter or margarine
2 cups chopped onion (about 3 medium)
1 cup chopped celery (about 2 stalks)
3 tablespoons flour
3 cups chicken stock or broth
8 ounces bottled clam juice
14 1/2 ounce can whole tomatoes, chopped (include juice)
4 cups peeled, diced potatoes (about 3 large)
1 1/2 pounds fresh turbot fillets, cut into 1" chunks (sole
        can also be used)
1 teaspoon salt
1/4 teaspoon pepper
1/2 teaspoon ground turmeric
2 teaspoons chopped, fresh parsley (or 1/2 teaspoon
        dried)

Melt butter in a large kettle. Cook onion and celery over medium heat until
golden. Sprinkle flour over, and cook, stirring, 2 minutes more. Add stock,
clam juice, tomatoes and potatoes. Bring to a boil, lower heat, cover, and
simmer 15 - 20 minutes or until potatoes are tender.

Add turbot, salt, pepper, turmeric and parsley and simmer 10 minutes more,
or until fish is easily flaked. Scrumptious! Sprinkle with oyster crackers if
you have some.

Chapter 12

MOM COOKS WITH HERBS

If you've never planted an herb garden,
pick a sunny spot and do it!
there's nothing more earthy and romantic
than snipping a fistful of fresh-from-the
garden herbs, and sprinkling them in a
variety of dishes ... with a little help
from Herb .

HERB'S ALL-PURPOSE HERB DIP

A creamy herb-packed dip with a hint of orange, that can be used on sandwiches in place of mayonnaise, in potato salad, dolloped on top of broiled fish or baked chicken or steamed broccoli or baked yams, and oh yes, as a regular old dip for munchies.

Makes about 1 1/2 cups

1/2 cup plain yogurt
1/2 cup sour cream
  2 tablespoons chopped fresh dill
  3 tablespoons chopped fresh chives
  2 tablespoons chopped fresh tarragon
  1 tablespoon minced shallot
  1 teaspoon freshly grated orange peel
1/2 teaspoon curry powder (optional)
1/2 teaspoon salt

Place all ingredients in a food processor with a steel blade. Process until herbs are flecks. Cover and refrigerate until needed.

IT'S GREAT FOR JUST ABOUT ANYTHING ... EXCEPT MAYBE TO WAX YOUR CAR!

HELLO I'M HERB

HERB'S FRIED PARSLEY

Crispy, batter-coated sprigs. Probably the only time you'll ever see parsley eaten on its own.

Serves 4 - 6 as a garnish

2 eggs
6 tablespoons flour
1/4 teaspoon salt
2 tablespoons water
Vegetable or peanut oil for deep frying
1 cup parsley sprigs, stems trimmed

Prepare the batter by beating the eggs in a medium bowl. Stir in the flour, salt and water until smooth.

In a medium skillet, heat the oil until a drop of batter browns quickly. Dip parsley sprigs in batter and carefully place in the hot oil (you might want to use a spoon), one at a time. When golden brown, remove with a slotted spoon and drain on paper towels. If needed, keep warm in a low oven. A nice touch parked next to a grilled steak.

FINALLY !
PARSLEY HAS
ITS DAY !

HERB'S THYME-STUFFED DRUMSTICKS

Baked in wine and garlic butter. You'd better make extra.

Serves 4

8 - 10 chicken drumsticks
16 - 20 small sprigs of fresh thyme (try lemon thyme, too)
1/2 cup dry white wine
4 tablespoons butter or margarine, melted
2 cloves garlic, minced
1/2 teaspoon salt

Preheat oven to 425 degrees. With your fingers, loosen the skin of the drumsticks from the bone end, without detaching it. Stuff each drumstick with 2 sprigs of thyme. Place in roasting pan and pour wine over. Bake, uncovered, 30 minutes, turning once. Drain off most of the liquid.

In the melted butter, stir in garlic and salt. Brush the drumsticks with half the butter mixture and return to oven. Turn oven to broil. Broil chicken 10 minutes more, or until browned and crispy. Remove from oven and brush on remaining garlic butter before serving. No silverware necessary.

HERB'S ROSEMARY LAMB STIR-FRY
With diced potatoes and cream, too.   Very fancy.

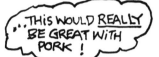

Serves 4

5 medium potatoes, peeled and diced (about 1/2")
1 cup chicken stock or broth
2 tablespoons butter or margarine
1 tablespoon vegetable oil
1 pound lean lamb meat, cut into thin strips
2 cloves garlic, minced
2 tablespoons fresh rosemary leaves, coarsely chopped
1/2 teaspoon salt
1/4 teaspoon pepper
1/2 cup heavy cream

Place potatoes in a large skillet and pour chicken stock over. Bring to a boil, lower heat, and simmer 10 minutes, or until potatoes are tender and liquid has almost disappeared. Add butter and margarine to skillet and lightly brown potatoes, making sure they don't burn. With a slotted spoon, remove to a bowl.

In same skillet, add lamb (pat dry with paper towels first), and stir-fry over medium-high heat 4 - 5 minutes, adding more oil if necessary. Lower heat, and add garlic, rosemary, salt, pepper and potatoes. Pour cream over and heat through.

HERB'S TOMATO-GRILLED PORK CHOPS with BASIL SAUCE

Tender and juicy, with such well-matched flavors.

Serves 6

1 1/2 tablespoons olive oil
1 tablespoon tomato paste
2 teaspoons Worcestershire sauce
1/2 teaspoon salt
1/2 teaspoon freshly ground black pepper
6 thick-cut (1 1/2") center pork chops

Basil Sauce:

2 tablespoons olive oil, divided
1 clove garlic, minced
2 scallions, sliced (include a little green)
3/4 cup loosely packed fresh basil leaves
2 tablespoons sour cream
1/4 teaspoon salt
1 tablespoon lemon juice

Preheat oven to broil. In a small bowl, whisk together olive oil, tomato paste, Worcestershire, salt and pepper. Brush chops on both sides with tomato mixture. Broil 12 minutes, turn, and broil 10 minutes more or just until insides are no longer pink.

Meanwhile, make basil sauce. In a small skillet, heat 1 tablespoon of oil and cook garlic and scallions over low heat until softened. Let cool slightly and place in a food processor with a steel blade. Add remaining ingredients (don't forget the rest of the oil), and process until smooth. Serve at room temperature on top of the hot chops.

143

HERB'S COTTAGE DILL BREAD

*Absolutely one of the finest breads known to man - and
using fresh dill makes all the difference in the world.*

Makes 1 loaf

1 package active dry yeast
3 tablespoons sugar, divided
1/4 cup warm (not hot) water
1 cup small curd cottage cheese
4 tablespoons butter
1 tablespoon minced onion
1 teaspoon salt
1/4 teaspoon baking soda
1 egg
3 tablespoons chopped, fresh dill
2 1/2 cups flour
A mixture of dill seed and coarse salt, optional

Dissolve yeast with 2 tablespoons of the sugar in warm water and let proof (get all bubbly) about 10 minutes. Place cottage cheese, butter, onion, salt and baking soda in a small saucepan and heat through, just until warm. In a large bowl, beat the egg and stir in the yeast mixture. Beat in cottage cheese mixture and flour to make a soft dough. Knead dough on floured surface 10 minutes or until springy. Place in a buttered bowl, turning to coat, and cover with a damp cloth. Put in a warm place and let rise 1 hour, or until doubled in size.

Punch dough down (the fun part) and shape into a loaf. Place in a buttered loaf pan (or you can use a 1 1/2 quart round casserole with bread shaped accordingly), and cover again with a damp towel. Let rise in a warm place for 30 - 40 minutes.

Preheat oven to 350 degrees. Bake bread for 30 minutes or until loaf is golden brown and slightly hollow sounding when tapped on the bottom. Remove from pan and cool on wire rack. While still warm, brush with melted butter and sprinkle with a combination of dill seeds and coarse salt.

A great bread to have baking if you're showing your house to prospective buyers.

HERB'S EXTRA CREAMY ROSEMARY MASHED POTATOES
A little something different for smasher lovers.

Serves 6

6 large Idaho potatoes, peeled and cut into large chunks
3 tablespoons sweet butter, softened
3 tablespoons light cream or half and half
2 tablespoons fresh rosemary leaves, minced
1/2 teaspoon salt
1/8 teaspoon ground white pepper

Place potato chunks in a large saucepan and cover with water. Boil about 15 minutes, or until fork tender. Remove from heat and drain water. Immediately add butter and cream to the hot potatoes and beat with an electric mixer until smooth. With a wooden spoon, stir in rosemary, salt and white pepper. Return potatoes to a very low heat and warm through, being careful not to scorch the bottom. You can put a pat of butter on the top of each serving, but I think they're fine just the way they are.

Chapter 13

There's nothing more pleasing than a tummy full of pasta.

RED-HOT ROTINI

Deep-fried, crunchy pasta coated with 5-alarm seasoning.
A munchy that requires liquid refreshment close at hand.

Makes about 4 1/2 cups worth

3 cups uncooked rotini (spiral pasta)
2 tablespoons vegetable oil plus more for deep frying
1 teaspoon ground coriander
1 teaspoon ground cumin
2 teaspoons salt
1 teaspoon cayenne pepper
1/4 teaspoon garlic powder
1/2 teaspoon turmeric
3 teaspoons dark sesame oil

Cook rotini according to package directions. Drain well without rinsing. Put pasta in a large bowl, add 2 tablespoons vegetable oil and toss to coat. Let cool, stirring occasionally.

In a large, deep skillet heat 1 1/2" vegetable oil until it passes the sizzle test. Fry rotini in three batches until lightly golden and crunchy, about 5 minutes per batch. Drain on paper towels and place back in the large bowl.

In a small bowl, mix together all dry spices. Toss pasta with sesame oil, add spice mixture, and turn to coat. Goes well with a game of gin rummy.

Store in tightly covered container in cupboard for up to a week.

MACARONI AND CHEESE AND CHEESE

Elbow macaroni in an onion-cream cheese sauce topped with sharp Cheddar and tomato slices. Pretty gourmet, if I do say so myself.

Serves 6 - 8

4 tablespoons butter or margarine, divided
1 medium onion, chopped
8 ounce package cream cheese
1 1/2 cups milk
1/4 cup Parmesan cheese (canned is fine)
1/2 teaspoon salt
8 ounce package elbow macaroni, cooked and drained
1 large tomato, sliced thin
2 cups grated sharp Cheddar cheese
1/3 cup seasoned, dry bread crumbs

CHEESE !?
...DID SOMEBODY
MENTION CHEESE ?

Preheat oven to 350 degrees. Butter a large casserole dish.

In a small skillet, melt 2 tablespoons of the butter and cook onion over medium heat until softened and just beginning to turn golden. Set aside.

In a large saucepan over low heat, melt cream cheese and milk, stirring until smooth. Stir in Parmesan cheese, salt and cooked onions. Fold in cooked macaroni. Pour in prepared casserole dish.

Arrange sliced tomatoes on top, then sprinkle Cheddar cheese on. Put bread crumbs on last. Dot with butter. Bake 25 - 30 minutes, uncovered. Delicious in the company of ham.

WHOLE WHEAT FETTUCINI with PINE NUTS

You may as well try some of these modern kinds of pasta.
You'll like my touch of cinnamon in this dish. Oh I know -
those pine nuts are awfully expensive. But they're so sweet
and buttery, it's worth the splurge once in a blue moon.

Serves 4

12 ounce package whole wheat fettucini
6 tablespoons butter or margarine
1 medium onion, chopped
2/3 cup pine nuts (about 1/4 pound)
1 teaspoon salt
1/2 teaspoon ground white pepper
1/4 teaspoon ground cinnamon
1/4 cup freshly grated Parmesan cheese

Cook fettucini according to package directions.

Meanwhile, melt butter in large, deep skillet. Over medium heat, cook onion until soft. Add pine nuts and cook, stirring, until golden. Add cooked, drained fettucini and lower heat. Add remaining ingredients and toss until well-mixed and heated through. Try it as a side dish, or with nothing more than a green salad.

DROP MEATBALLS 'n MACARONI in CREAMY BEEF SAUCE
Melt-in-your-mouth meatballs that require no rolling - happily smothered in a light sauce and tossed with macaroni.

Serves 4 - 6

Meatballs:
1 1/2 pounds ground beef chuck or round
2 tablespoons tomato paste
4 cloves garlic, minced
1/4 cup grated Parmesan cheese
1/2 cup dry bread crumbs
1 teaspoon salt
1/2 teaspoon pepper
2 eggs
1/4 cup milk

2 cups inexpensive white wine
2 tablespoons cornstarch
2 cups beef stock or broth
1/2 cup light cream
8 ounces elbow macaroni, cooked and drained

Make meatballs by mixing all meatball ingredients in a large bowl. Mixture will be soft.

In a large, deep skillet, bring wine to a simmer. Pinch teaspoonfuls of meat mixture and drop into wine (use both hands and do two at a time). Let simmer 10 minutes, uncovered. Gently turn and cook another 10 - 15 minutes. Pour off most of remaining liquid. Dissolve cornstarch in beef stock and add to skillet. Simmer about 5 minutes, or until slightly thickened. Pour in cream and add cooked macaroni. Toss well, heat through, and serve with enthusiasm.

CHOO CHOO WHEELS and CHICKEN LIVERS

Crispy bacon and caramelized onions team up with tender chicken livers for a treat I would have seconds on and skip dessert.

Serves 4 - 6

4 tablespoons sweet butter
2 medium onions, sliced thin
3 slices bacon
1 1/2 pound chicken livers, trimmed of fat
Flour for dredging, seasoned with salt and pepper
2 cloves garlic, minced
1 cup chicken stock or broth
8 ounces Choo Choo Wheels, cooked and drained

In a large skillet, melt butter and cook onions until lightly browned. Remove with slotted spoon. In same skillet, cook bacon until crisp and drain on paper towels. Coat chicken livers in flour and lightly brown in bacon fat, turning once. Add garlic, stock, caramelized onions, crumbled bacon and Choo Choo Wheels. Simmer just for a few minutes, or until you can't wait any longer.

153

RIGATONI with MOM'S SECRET MEAT SAUCE
A pleasing tomato-meat sauce with (don't tell anyone) coffee.

Serves 6 - 8

1 1/2 pounds ground beef round
1 medium onion, chopped
1 quart canned tomatoes, crushed (include juice)
1 1/2 teaspoons salt
1/2 teaspoon pepper
1/2 teaspoon sugar
1 tablespoon dried basil leaves
1/4 cup canned Parmesan cheese
1/4 teaspoon crushed red pepper flakes
12 ounce can tomato paste
1 tablespoon instant coffee dissolved in 1 cup warm
water
1 cup heavy cream
16 ounces rigatoni noodles, cooked and drained

In a large pot, brown meat. Drain any fat. Add onions and cook, stirring 1 minute. Add tomatoes, salt, pepper, sugar, basil, Parmesan, pepper flakes, tomato paste and coffee water. Simmer over low flame, uncovered, 30 minutes, stirring occasionally. Stir in cream and simmer 5 minutes more. Spoon sauce over cooked rigatoni and play Stump the Family.

PORK CABBAGE NOODLES

*An old favorite, made into a main course with strips of
pork tenderloin and a sprinkling of caraway seeds.*

Serves 6

6 tablespoons butter or margarine
2 large onions, chopped
1 pound pork tenderloin, cut into thin strips
1/2 head cabbage, coarsely chopped
8 ounces broad egg noodles
1/2 teaspoon caraway seeds
1 teaspoon salt
1/2 teaspoon ground white pepper

Melt butter in large skillet and cook onions over medium-high heat until just beginning to soften. Add pork and cook about 5 minutes, or until no longer pink.

Stir in cabbage, cover and cook over low heat until cabbage is tender, about 10 minutes. Add noodles and seasonings, toss well, and heat through before serving.

...THIS COULD BE OUR SHOT AT THE BIGTIME

CHICKEN and MUSHROOMS over THIN SPAGHETTI with SOUR CREAM-BASIL SAUCE

My word. The ingredients are all but
listed in the recipe title. You get the picture.

Serves 4 - 6

4 tablespoons butter or margarine
1/2 Spanish onion, chopped
2 skinless, boneless chicken breasts, cut into bite-sized
   pieces
1/2 pound mushrooms, sliced thin
1/2 cup loosely packed fresh basil leaves, chopped
1 teaspoon salt
1/4 teaspoon pepper
16 ounces sour cream mixed with 1/4 cup milk
16 ounces thin spaghetti, cooked and drained

In a large skillet, melt butter and cook onion 4 minutes over medium heat. Add chicken pieces and cook 6 -8 minutes more, stirring. Add mushrooms, basil, salt and pepper and cook 3 - 4 minutes. Finally, lower heat and add sour cream mixture and simmer 10 minutes, uncovered. Gently fold in cooked spaghetti and heat through.

USE YOUR NOODLE!!

STOVE PIPES 'n PEPPER STEAK

Big, fat stove pipe pasta sharing the plate with green pepper and thyme, in a simple beef sauce. Hearty fare.

Serves 4

3 tablespoons butter or margarine
2 tablespoons olive oil
2 medium onions, chopped
2 beef chuck shoulder steaks, trimmed and cut into strips
2 green bell peppers, cut into strips
2 cups beef stock or broth
1/2 teaspoon ground thyme
1 teaspoon salt
1/2 teaspoon pepper
2 tablespoons cornstarch dissolved in 2 tablespoons cold water
8 ounces stove pipes, cooked and drained

Heat butter and oil in a large, deep skillet. Cook onion over medium heat until softened. Add steak strips and cook 5 minutes, stirring occasionally. Add green pepper strips and cook 5 minutes more. Pour in beef stock along with thyme, salt and pepper and bring to a simmer. Stir in cornstarch mixture. When slightly thickened, add stove pipes and toss until heated through.

CINNAMON NOODLE PUDDING SQUARES

*Visions of grandmothers come to mind with this nostalgic dish.
It seems to hit the spot in early Spring, when there's still
a nip in the air, and the smell of cinnamon fills the kitchen.*

Serves 8

8 ounces medium noodles
4 tablespoons butter or margarine, melted
1/2 pound cottage cheese
1 egg, beaten
1/2 cup brown sugar
1 teaspoon vanilla extract
1 teaspoon ground cinnamon

Preheat oven to 375 degrees. Butter a 9" x 13" baking pan.

Boil noodles 5 minutes, or 2 minutes less than package instructions. Drain and set aside.

In a large bowl, combine remaining ingredients, mixing well. Fold in cooked noodles. Pour mixture into prepared pan and bake 40 - 45 minutes or until top is browned. Let rest 10 minutes before cutting into squares. Best eaten at room temperature with a cup of hot, black coffee in front of the fireplace, for one of the last fires of the season.

Chapter 14

MOM GOES NUTS

Munchies, main courses, side dishes, and sweets:
we all have to go nuts every now and then.

BARBECUED ALMONDS

Toasted almonds in a not-too-spicy coating
to fill the nut dish when company comes.

Makes 2 cups

1 tablespoon butter or margarine
2 tablespoons Worcestershire sauce
1 teaspoon ketchup
1/4 teaspoon cayenne pepper
2 cups blanched, whole almonds
Salt to taste

Preheat oven to 400 degrees.

Melt butter in a medium saucepan over low heat. Mix in Worcestershire sauce, ketchup and cayenne pepper. Stir in almonds and coat well.

Spread almonds on a baking sheet. Toast in oven 12 - 14 minutes, stirring several times to prevent burning. Drain on paper towels and sprinkle with a little salt. Best if eaten warm from the oven. Store in tightly covered container at room temperature if you actually have any leftovers.

...IS IT HOT IN HERE, OR IS IT JUST ME?

CASHEW CHICKEN

Dipped in buttermilk, coated in cashews,
and baked to a golden brown.

Serves 6

1/2 cup (1 stick) butter or margarine
1 cup buttermilk
1 egg, beaten
1 1/2 cups ground cashews (do it in the food processor
using the steel blade)
1/2 cup flour
1 teaspoon salt
6 chicken breast halves

Preheat oven to 350 degrees. Put butter in a roasting pan and melt in oven (4 - 5 minutes). Remove from oven and set aside.

Whisk buttermilk and egg together in a shallow dish. In another shallow dish, mix together ground cashews, flour and salt.

Dip chicken pieces in buttermilk mixture, then coat with cashew mixture. Place in roasting pan, turning to coat with melted butter.

Bake chicken, uncovered, 1 hour and 10 minutes, or until golden brown. Add more melted butter to pan if needed, but you should be fine.

WALNUT CREAM BISCUITS
Easy, fluffy cookie-cutter biscuits with
just an inkling of sweetness. Boundless uses.

Makes 12

2 cups flour
1/2 teaspoon salt
1 tablespoon baking powder
1 1/2 teaspoons sugar
1/2 cup coarsely chopped walnuts
1 cup heavy cream

Preheat oven to 425 degrees. Lightly butter a baking sheet.

In a large bowl, combine flour, salt, baking powder, sugar and walnuts. Pour in cream and mix lightly, just until blended (overmixing makes tough biscuits).

Place dough on a lightly floured surface and knead until smooth. Press to 1/2" thickness. With a 3" round cookie cutter, cut 12 biscuits. Place on prepared baking sheet and bake 12 - 15 minutes, or until lightly golden. Serve warm with butter. A little jam hits the spot.

MIXED-NUT CHICKEN-FRIED STEAK

Sinfully delicious - cream gravy included.

Serves 4

4 boneless top sirloin steaks, 1/4" thick (about 1 1/2 pounds)
2 eggs
1/2 cup flour
1 cup finely chopped mixed nuts (do it in the food processor using steel blade)
Peanut oil for frying
2/3 cup light cream

Prepare steaks by pounding thin with a meat mallet.

In one shallow dish, beat the eggs. In another, combine the flour and the mixed nuts.

In a large, deep skillet heat 1/2" peanut oil until it passes the sizzle test. Coat steaks first in the egg, then in the nut mixture. Fry in hot oil until browned on both sides, turning just once.

Remove steaks from skillet and keep warm. Discard oil, leaving all those brown thingies in the bottom of the skillet. Add the cream and boil about 2 minutes, scraping bottom. Top each steak with a spoonful of cream gravy.

164

FRESH PEA PODS and ALMONDS in BROWN BUTTER

There's nothing like the taste of crisp-tender pea pods -
except when they're joined by almonds and a smidgen of garlic.

Serves 4

4 tablespoons sweet butter
1/2 cup slivered, blanched almonds
1 pound fresh pea pods, ends trimmed
1 clove garlic, minced
1/2 teaspoon salt

Over low heat, melt butter in large skillet until it starts turning brown. Add almonds and cook, stirring, until golden. Stir in pea pods, garlic and salt and cook, tossing 3 - 4 minutes, or until pea pods are crisp-tender.

CHOCOLATE-MACADAMIA CHEESECAKE SQUARES

Almost like a bar cookie, they have just enough cheesecake
without their sticking to the roof of your mouth like some do.

Makes 16

Bottom crust:
1/4 cup firmly packed brown sugar
1 cup crushed chocolate wafer cookies (about 25)
1/2 cup flour
6 tablespoons butter or margarine, melted

8 ounces cream cheese, softened
1/4 cup sugar
1 egg
1 tablespoon lemon juice
2 tablespoons light cream
1 teaspoon vanilla extract
3 1/2 ounce jar macadamia nuts, chopped

Preheat oven to 350 degrees. In a medium bowl, combine brown sugar, wafer crumbs and flour. Stir in melted butter and mix with hands until crumbly. Reserve 1 cup for topping. Press the rest into the bottom of an 8" square pan. Bake 12 - 15 minutes or until set.

In a medium bowl, beat cream cheese with sugar until smooth. Add egg, lemon juice, cream and vanilla and mix thoroughly. Fold in nuts.
Pour into baked crust and sprinkle top with reserved crumb mixture. Return to oven and bake 25 minutes. Cool completely before cutting into 2" squares. Store in refrigerator.

PISTACHIO-PEANUT BRITTLE

You won't feel like your teeth will break with my version - it melts in your mouth and the green from the pistachios adds a touch of color.

Makes enough for both you and someone you work with

2 cups sugar
1 cup light corn syrup
1 cup shelled natural pistachio nuts (not red)
1 cup salted peanuts
1 teaspoon baking soda
2 tablespoons sweet butter
1/2 teaspoon vanilla extract

Generously butter a 11" x 17" baking pan with sides.

In a large, heavy saucepan, cook sugar and corn syrup over medium heat, 20 - 25 minutes, stirring occasionally as it bubbles. When it is a light golden color, add both nuts and cook 3 - 5 minutes more until mixture is a deep caramel color.

Remove from heat and stir in baking soda, butter, and vanilla (mixture will turn opaque and bubble up). Pour onto prepared baking sheet and spread out with a wooden spoon, making sure not to burn yourself - it's hot! Let dry at room temperature for about an hour. Carve out the first piece with a sharp knife, and break up the rest with your hands. Store in tightly sealed container so it doesn't get sticky.

NUM NUM

Chapter 15

DIXIE FIXINS'

Pull up a rocking chair and enjoy a complete menu with shades of the south ... from fried chicken all the way down to pecan pound cake.

SPOON CORNBREAD

A cake-like bread made with white cornmeal and buttermilk and baked in a casserole dish. Scoop a spoonful out and paint with a little butter. Mmmmm.

Serves 6

2 tablespoons butter
3/4 cup white cornmeal
1/2 teaspoon baking soda
1/2 teaspoon salt
1/2 teaspoon sugar
1 1/2 cups buttermilk
1 egg, beaten

Preheat oven to 400 degrees. Place butter in a one quart casserole dish and melt it in the oven.

In a medium bowl, combine cornmeal, soda, salt and sugar. Stir in buttermilk, then egg.

Pour mixture into buttered casserole dish and bake 30 minutes or until golden. Serve with butter and maybe a little homemade peach jam.

TWELVE OAKS SOUTHERN FRIED CHICKEN
with CREAM GRAVY

You won't find two southerners that agree on the best way to fry up a batch of chicken. Truth be known, they're all great - especially this recipe...bathed in salted milk and eggs, dipped in plain old flour and fried in peanut oil 'til crispy. It seems only right to use a big ole black wrought iron skillet for this one.

Serves 6

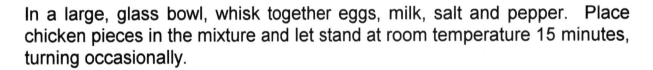

2 eggs
1 cup milk
2 teaspoons salt
1 teaspoon pepper
6 split chicken breasts
About 3 cups peanut oil, or enough to fill 1/3 of the skillet
1 1/4 cups flour
1 cup heavy cream

In a large, glass bowl, whisk together eggs, milk, salt and pepper. Place chicken pieces in the mixture and let stand at room temperature 15 minutes, turning occasionally.

In a large black wrought iron skillet, heat peanut oil until it passes the sizzle test.

Coat each chicken piece generously with flour and fry, 3 at a time, meaty side down for 15 minutes over medium heat. Turn with tongs and fry 5 minutes more. Keep first batch in a warm oven until all are done.

After the pan cools down a bit, discard peanut oil, leaving 2 tablespoons worth in the skillet. Turn heat to medium, add cream, and let it bubble for about 3 minutes. You can add a pinch of salt to the cream if it suits you. Spoon cream over fried chicken before feasting.

HOT MAMMY CHEESE GRITS

Creamy grits and Cheddar cheese, livened a bit with hot peppers.

Serves 6

2 cups milk
1 cup water
1 cup quick-cooking grits
3 tablespoons butter or margarine
1 Jalapeno pepper, seeded and finely chopped
1 clove garlic, minced
1/2 teaspoon salt
1/2 teaspoon pepper
2 cups shredded Cheddar cheese

In a large saucepan, combine all ingredients except the cheese. Cook, uncovered, about 30 minutes, stirring frequently. The liquid should be all soaked up in the grits.

Add cheese and stir just until melted. Like mashed potatoes to a southerner.

*The addition of pickled beets turns an ordinary coleslaw
into the tastiest, prettiest bright pink slaw this side of the Mississippi.*

Serves 6

1/2 large head cabbage
2 medium carrots
16 ounce jar sliced pickled beets
2/3 cup mayonnaise
2 tablespoons honey
1/2 teaspoon salt

Using the shredding attachment of a food processor, shred cabbage, then carrots. Remove to large bowl.

Drain beets, reserving 3 tablespoons of the juice. Slice beets into strips and add to the cabbage mixture.

In a small bowl, mix together the reserved beet juice, mayonnaise, honey and salt. Pour over vegetables and toss well.

SOUTHERN COMFORT-PECAN POUND CAKE

Made moist by sour cream - and glazed with bourbon icing.

Makes 1 bundt cake

1 cup (2 sticks) butter, softened
2 1/2 cups sugar
6 eggs
3 cups sifted cake flour
2 teaspoons baking powder
1 teaspoon salt
1 cup sour cream
1/2 cup bourbon whiskey
1 1/2 cups coarsely chopped pecans

Glaze:
2 cups sifted confectioners' sugar
2 tablespoons bourbon whiskey
4 tablespoons butter, melted
2 - 3 tablespoons water

Preheat oven to 325 degrees. Butter a bundt or tube pan.

In a food processor using steel blade, cream butter and sugar. Beat in eggs. Combine flour, baking powder and salt and add to the mixture 1/3 at a time, alternating with sour cream mixed with bourbon. Quickly fold in pecans. Pour batter in prepared pan and bake 1 hour and 10 minutes, or until it passes the toothpick test. Let cake cool 15 minutes before turning out on wire rack.

To make glaze: Mix together sugar and bourbon. Stir while adding melted butter. Add just enough water to make a pourable glaze. Place cake on a pretty plate and spoon glaze over, letting it run down the sides. Best if eaten just a teensy bit warm. Not bad for breakfast, either.

Chapter 16

THE POT ROAST CHAPTER

Tom Wilson's favorite food in the world is pot roast.
Now his own personal recipe is yours to taste.
— I'll take credit for the noodles though.

TOM'S GOOD OLD POT ROAST with HOMEMADE NOODLES

Studded with cloves and baked in beef stock until it falls apart. Not without, of course; onions, carrots and potatoes - and turnips just to be different. The hand-cut noodles cook right in the pan and the flour from them automatically thickens the gravy. Comfort food at its best.

Serves 6

Noodles:
- 4 egg yolks
- 4 tablespoons water
- 1 teaspoon salt
- 2 cups flour (approximately)

- 4 pound beef chuck roast rubbed with salt and pepper
- Flour for dredging
- 3 tablespoons vegetable oil
- 6 - 8 whole cloves
- 2 bay leaves
- 6 cups beef stock or broth
- 4 turnips (about 1 pound), peeled and chunked
- 4 small, yellow onions, peeled and chunked
- 4 large Idaho potatoes (2 1/2 pounds), peeled and chunked
- 1 bunch carrots (about 6), scraped and cut into 2" pieces

Make noodles: In a medium bowl, beat egg yolks with a fork. Stir in water and salt. Slowly blend in flour with hands until dough is somewhat dry but still pliable. Roll out on floured surface as thin as you possibly can. Dry a few hours, turning occasionally.

Make pot roast: Preheat oven to 350 degrees. Dredge seasoned roast in flour. On top of the stove, heat oil in one of those big, pot roast-type roasting pans, and brown meat on both sides. Remove from heat.

Stud the top of the roast with cloves and lay bay leaves on. Pour beef stock over, cover, and cook 1 1/2 hours. Add all vegetables to the pot and cook another hour, covered. Remove cloves and bay leaves and discard.

With a sharp knife, cut noodle dough into strips and add to the meat and vegetables. Recover, and cook 30 minutes more, until noodles are tender.

Cut meat into serving-sized portions, and place on individual plates. Surround with vegetables and noodles, and spoon gravy on top. Season with salt and pepper as desired.

Tom's recommendation for dessert: Good quality butter pecan ice cream topped with chocolate syrup.

Chapter 17

MOM'S APPLE PIES

Seems like everyone knows how to make an all-American apple pie. Add a little excitement by trying my versions... six variations on a classic.

Make filling: In a large bowl, combine sugar and cornstarch. Add apple butter, eggs, milk and cream. Mix well. Pour into pie crust and bake 55 - 60 minutes, or just until set. Let cool completely before serving.

You can top it with whipped cream, but I like it wedded with coffee ice cream.

GOLDEN APPLE CUSTARD PIE
A cheerful, sunshine-yellow pie -
rich and creamy and pretty to look at.

Makes 1 9" pie

1 tablespoon butter or margarine, softened
9" deep-dish pie crust, unbaked
2 large, Golden Delicious apples, cored and sliced
3 eggs
1 1/2 cups milk
1/2 cup light cream or half and half
1 teaspoon vanilla extract
1/2 cup sugar, divided
1/2 teaspoon ground nutmeg
1/2 teaspoon salt

Preheat oven to 400 degrees. Butter the bottom of the pie crust and arrange apple slices in an overlapping pinwheel design. In a large bowl, blend together eggs, milk, cream, vanilla and all but 2 teaspoons of the sugar. Carefully spoon mixture over the apples. Mix remaining sugar with nutmeg and salt and sprinkle on top.

Place pie in a roasting pan and pour boiling water to reach halfway up the side of the pie. Place in oven and bake 40 minutes. Reduce oven temperature to 300 degrees and bake 20 minutes more, or until custard is set. Cool completely before slicing. Store in refrigerator.

GRANNY SMITH CHOCOLATE OATMEAL PIE
A splendid concoction of flavors and texture - ambrosia!

Makes 1 9" pie

4 eggs
1 cup sugar
2 tablespoons flour
1 teaspoon cinnamon
1/8 teaspoon salt
2 tablespoons melted butter
1/2 cup light corn syrup
1/2 cup honey
1 teaspoon vanilla extract
1 cup oats
2 Granny Smith apples, peeled, cored and chopped
1/2 cup semi-sweet chocolate chips
9" deep dish pie crust, unbaked

Preheat oven to 350 degrees.

In a large bowl, beat eggs until frothy. In a separate small bowl, mix together flour, cinnamon and salt. Stir into eggs until blended.

Add butter, corn syrup, honey and vanilla and blend. Fold in oatmeal, apples and chocolate chips. Pour into pie crust and bake 1 hour and 10 minutes, or until pie is set. Let cool before slicing. A glass of cold milk is the only accessory you'll need.

APPLE MERINGUE PIE
Light and tangy - piled a mile high with no-fail meringue.

Makes one 9" deep-dish pie

9" deep dish pie crust, unbaked
3 egg yolks (save whites for meringue)
1/2 cup apple juice concentrate
6 tablespoons cornstarch
2 cups cold water
1/3 cup sugar
3 tablespoons butter, melted
2 teaspoons cider vinegar
1 teaspoon vanilla extract

Meringue: 1 tablespoon cornstarch
1/2 cup cold water
3 egg whites, room temperature
6 tablespoons sugar
1/8 teaspoon salt
1/2 teaspoon vanilla extract
Ground cinnamon

Bake pie crust according to package directions. Let cool.

In a medium bowl, mix together egg yolks, apple juice, cornstarch mixed with the water and sugar. Place mixture in the top of a double boiler over hot, not boiling water. Cook 30 minutes, or until thickened, stirring frequently. Remove from heat and stir in butter, vinegar and vanilla. Pour into baked pie shell and let cool.

Preheat oven to 350 degrees.

Make meringue: In a small saucepan, combine cornstarch and water. Cook over medium heat, stirring constantly until thickened and clear, about 4 minutes. Cool completely.

In a large, non-plastic bowl, beat egg whites with electric mixer until foamy. Continue beating while slowly adding sugar, and beat until stiff. Beat in salt, vanilla and cornstarch mixture. With a rubber spatula, spread meringue over cooled pie. Bake 15 minutes until meringue is nicely browned. Let cool, then refrigerate until ready to eat.

Chapter 18

MOM'S WORLD TOUR

A quick trip around the world to discover comfort foods from afar.

SCOTCH EGGS

Hard-boiled eggs, blanketed in pork sausage, breaded and fried until golden. An appetizer, a breakfast dish, a lunch treat, an accent to a dinner.

Serves 4 - 8

8 hard-boiled eggs, peeled
Flour for dredging
1 pound bulk pork sausage
3/4 cup dry bread crumbs
1/4 teaspoon mace
1 teaspoon salt
1/4 teaspoon pepper
1 egg, beaten
Vegetable oil for deep-frying
Brown mustard, optional

Dredge eggs in flour. Divide sausage into 8 portions. Flatten each sausage portion and form around egg to coat.

In a small bowl, mix together bread crumbs, mace, salt and pepper.

Dip sausage eggs into beaten egg, then coat with seasoned bread crumbs.

Heat about 1 1/2" oil in large, deep skillet until it passes the sizzle test. Fry coated eggs in two batches until deep golden brown, about 6 - 8 minutes. Drain well on paper towels and serve warm with a dollop of spicy mustard on the side.

TURKISH LAMB and ONION KABOBS
Grilled in a lemon-oregano marinade.

Serves 3 - 4

1/3 cup freshly squeezed lemon juice (about 3 lemons)
2 tablespoons olive oil
2 teaspoons salt
1/4 teaspoon pepper
1 tablespoon fresh oregano leaves, coarsely chopped
2 1/2 pound lamb leg, trimmed and cut into 1 1/2" cubes
3 medium yellow onions, peeled and quartered

In a large glass bowl, whisk together lemon juice, olive oil, salt, pepper and oregano. Add lamb, toss to coat, and refrigerate several hours, turning occasionally. Reserve marinade.

Preheat oven to broil.

Alternately skewer about 4 - 5 pieces of lamb and 2 pieces of onion on each of 6 metal skewers. Brush with about half of the marinade.

Broil 8 minutes on top rack, turn and broil 5 minutes more, brushing with remaining marinade. The kids get one, the adults get two.

INDIAN CHICKEN WINGS with APPLE YOGURT DIP

*A new twist to the traditional Buffalo wings. Exotically
spicy with a refreshing dip to calm the fires.*

Serves 6 (4 wings each)

24 chicken wings
1/3 cup flour
3 teaspoons cayenne pepper, divided
Vegetable oil for deep-frying
1 cup plain yogurt
1 teaspoon ground cumin
1/2 teaspoon ground coriander
1/2 teaspoon turmeric
1/4 teaspoon cinnamon
1 teaspoon salt

Dip:
1 cup plain yogurt
1/2 teaspoon grated fresh ginger root
1/2 teaspoon salt
1/2 sour apple (like a Granny Smith)

Tuck tips of wings behind meaty part for a more compact wing. In a medium bowl, combine flour and 2 teaspoons of the cayenne pepper.

Heat about 1 1/2" oil in a large, deep skillet. Coat wings in flour mixture and fry over medium-high heat in several batches, about 15 - 20 minutes, or until crispy. Drain on paper towels. When all are cooked, discard all but 2 tablespoons of the oil. Return wings to skillet.

In a small bowl, combine yogurt, cumin, coriander, turmeric, cinnamon, salt and the remaining 1 teaspoon cayenne pepper.

Pour yogurt mixture over wings, toss to coat, cover and simmer 10 minutes.

While wings are simmering, make apple-yogurt dip: In a small bowl, combine yogurt, ginger root and salt. Just before serving, grate apple into dip and mix.

HUNGARIAN GOULASH with AUSTRIAN POTATO DUMPLINGS

A big pot of tender beef chunks in a savory tomato-paprika sauce with big, tasty dumplings floating on the top like clouds.

Serves 8

8 tablespoons butter or margarine, divided
2 large onions, chopped
3 tablespoons Hungarian paprika (imported has best
    flavor)
2 teaspoons salt
1 teaspoon black pepper
3 pound beef chuck roast
4 cups water
2 cups chicken stock or broth
2 large tomatoes, diced

Dumplings: 3 large potatoes, peeled and quartered
1/4 cup (1/2 stick) butter, softened
2 eggs
2 teaspoons salt
1/8 teaspoon ground nutmeg
2 cups flour

In a large, heavy pot with a lid, melt 6 tablespoons of the butter over medium heat. Add onions and cook, stirring, until just beginning to brown. With a slotted spoon, remove to a bowl and set aside.

Combine paprika, salt and pepper in medium bowl. Cut meat into 1 1/2" cubes and roll in paprika mixture. Melt remaining 2 tablespoons butter in the pot, add meat, and brown on all sides. Return onion to pot, along with water and chicken stock. Bring to a boil, cover and simmer on low heat 1 1/2 hours. Add tomatoes and simmer 30 minutes more.

Make dumplings: Boil potato chunks until tender, about 20 minutes. Drain water, add butter, and mash with a fork while still hot. Mix in eggs, salt, nutmeg and flour. Form into dumplings the size of plums.

With a large spoon, carefully place dumplings in pot with goulash. Cover and simmer 15 minutes. Enjoy with relish (not the pickle kind, the emotional kind).

AHHHH... I RELISH THAT GOULASH...
URP!

CHINESE SHRIMP FRIED RICE

Fluffy white rice, stir-fried with bits of shrimp, mushrooms and shreds of egg in a mildly sweetened soy sauce.
Can be a mein course (Chinese humor) or a side dish.

Serves 6

1 1/2 cups raw white rice
2 1/2 cups water
4 tablespoons peanut or vegetable oil
3 eggs
1 teaspoon salt
1 1/2 pounds raw shrimp, shelled, cleaned and coarsely chopped
3 medium onions, chopped
1/4 pound mushrooms, sliced
4 tablespoons soy sauce
1 teaspoon sugar

Combine rice with water in a large saucepan with a lid. Bring to a boil, lower heat, cover and cook until rice is tender and water is absorbed, about 15 minutes. Set aside.

In a large skillet or wok, heat the oil. Break the eggs into it, breaking the yolk and fry until firm. Turn and fry 1 minute more. Remove pan from heat and cut the eggs into long, thin shreds. Return the skillet to the stove, add salt, pepper, shrimp, onions and mushrooms. Cook, stirring, over medium heat about 5 minutes, until shrimp turns pink. Stir in cooked rice, soy sauce and sugar and cook 5 - 7 minutes more, tossing occasionally. Serve with more soy sauce.

PERUVIAN POTATO PIE

Mashed potatoes layered with sautéed tomatoes and Cheddar cheese, crowned with a fluffy, golden egg topping. This is a variation of a favorite enjoyed high up in the mountains of Peru.

Serves 8 - 9

3 large potatoes (about 2 pounds), peeled and chunked
1 teaspoon salt
3 tablespoons olive oil
1 large onion, finely chopped
2 cloves garlic, minced
2 large tomatoes, peeled and chopped (plunge into boiling
      water 15 seconds to easily remove skin)
1/2 pound sharp Cheddar cheese, thinly sliced
2 eggs, separated
2 tablespoons heavy cream

Preheat oven to 350 degrees. Butter a 9" square baking pan or casserole.

In a large saucepan, boil potatoes until tender, about 15 minutes. Drain well, add salt, and mash with a fork. Set aside.

In a medium skillet, heat oil. Cook onion and garlic until soft. Add tomato and simmer, stirring, until most of liquid is gone, about 8 minutes.

Spoon half the mashed potatoes into the prepared baking dish, gently pressing to flatten. Spread half the tomato mixture over the potatoes, then arrange half the cheese slices on top. Make another potato layer, followed again by the tomatoes and the cheese.

Whisk together the egg yolks with the cream. With an electric mixer, beat the egg whites until soft peaks form. Fold the egg yolk mixture into the whites. Spoon over potato pie. Bake 1 hour or until golden brown. Serve as a side dish with nearly anything.

GREEK FRIED EGGPLANT with GARLIC SAUCE
Crispy, golden rounds dipped in a very appropriate garlic sauce with almonds. Grecian "potato chips".

Serves 6

Garlic sauce: 3 cloves garlic, smashed with the flat side of a
                     chopping knife
              1 medium potato, peeled and boiled until tender (or
                     microwaved until done)
         1/4 cup blanched, ground almonds
          1 cup olive oil
         3 tablespoons tarragon vinegar
        1/2 teaspoon salt
        1/4 teaspoon ground white pepper

        2 medium eggplants, sliced 1/4" thick
        Salt
        Vegetable oil for deep frying
        Flour for dredging

Make garlic sauce: In a food processor using steel blade, put garlic, potato and almonds. Process until smooth. With processor running, slowly add oil and vinegar, alternating, until sauce is the consistency of mayonnaise. Season with salt and pepper. Refrigerate, covered, until ready to use.

Arrange eggplant slices upright in a large colander and salt liberally. Let stand at least 30 minutes, over a plate or the sink to catch drippings.

In a large, deep skillet, heat about 1" oil until it passes the sizzle test. Pat eggplant slices dry with paper towels, dredge in flour and fry in hot oil until golden brown, turning once. Fry in several batches, draining on paper towels as they come out of the pan. Keep warm in a low oven until all are done. Serve with garlic sauce either as a side dish or an appetizer.

FINNISH MUSHROOM SALAD

*Fresh mushrooms tossed in chilled cream with
dill and chives - all white and pretty.*

Serves 4 - 6

1 pound fresh, white mushrooms, trimmed and sliced
3/4 cup heavy whipping cream, divided
1 teaspoon sugar
2 tablespoons chopped, fresh chives (or 1/2 teaspoon
     dried)
1 tablespoon chopped, fresh dill (or 1/2 teaspoon dried)
1/2 teaspoon salt
1/8 teaspoon ground white pepper

Place mushrooms in a medium salad bowl.

In a small bowl, whip 1/2 cup of the cream along with the sugar, with an electric mixer until soft peaks form. Fold in chives, dill, salt and pepper. Pour over mushrooms and toss gently. Pour remaining 1/4 cup cream, unwhipped, over mushrooms and mix again.

Serve immediately or refrigerate until ready to serve. Try not to make it more than a few hours before serving.

HEY !
...THIS COULD BE
THE FINNISH
FOR US !

JAMAICAN BANANA PUDDING
with COFFEE-RUM WHIPPED CREAM

Individual baked banana custards - topped with a mound of spiked coffee whipped cream. Makes you think of a postcard beach with no one on it.

Serves 6

Pudding:
  5 very ripe, medium bananas, peeled and chunked
  1 egg
  3 tablespoons banana liqueur
  1 cup heavy cream
  1 teaspoon lemon juice

Topping:
  1/2 cup heavy whipping cream
  1 tablespoon sugar
  3/4 teaspoon instant coffee, dissolved in 1/2 teaspoon warm water
  1 tablespoon dark rum

Preheat oven to 300 degrees. Butter six custard cups, 1/2 - 3/4 cup size.

Make pudding: In a food processor using steel blade, place bananas, egg, banana liqueur, cream and lemon juice. Blend until smooth.

Divide banana mixture into prepared custard cups. Set cups in a roasting pan and pour boiling water to come halfway up the sides of the custard cups. Bake 30 minutes or until pudding is set. Let stand 15 minutes.

Make topping: In a small, deep bowl, whip cream with electric mixer until soft peaks form. Slowly add sugar, continuing to beat until stiff peaks form. Fold in coffee and rum. Unmold pudding and smother with topping.

SPANISH ORANGE-CARAMEL FLAN
Caramelized sugar tops this smooth, orange-zested custard.

Serves 4

Caramel top: 1/2 cup sugar

Flan: 3 eggs
                 1 tablespoon grated orange peel
                 12 ounce can evaporated milk
                 1/3 cup sugar
                 1 teaspoon vanilla extract
                 1 teaspoon almond extract
                 Pinch salt

Preheat oven to 350 degrees.

Make caramel: In a small, heavy saucepan, heat sugar over low heat, stirring, until melted and golden brown. Divide among four 3/4 - 1 cup custard cups. Quickly turn cups to coat bottom and a little up the sides. Let stand a few minutes until hardened.

Make flan: Mix together all flan ingredients in a large bowl. Divide among coated custard cups. Place cups in roasting pan and pour boiling water to come halfway up the sides of the cups.

Bake 1 hour, or until they pass the toothpick test. Let cool, then refrigerate until chilled. To unmold, dip bottoms of cups in a bowl of hot water, loosen edges with a knife, and transfer to individual dessert plates.

Chapter 19

CHEZ MOM'S (FANCY FRENCH GRUB)

A five-course meal featuring dishes that made France famous. Served Liner-style.

CHICKEN LIVER PATE (FANCY LIVER SPREAD)
Extra buttery, with a dash of garlic and a splash of brandy.

Makes about 1 1/2 cups

3 tablespoons butter or margarine
1 pound chicken livers, trimmed of fat
2 cloves garlic, minced
1/4 cup chopped onion (about 1/2 of a small onion)
1 teaspoon salt
1/2 teaspoon ground white pepper
1 teaspoon dry mustard
1/2 cup (1 stick) sweet butter, softened
1 tablespoon brandy

Heat 3 tablespoons butter in a medium skillet. Add chicken livers, garlic and onion. Cook over medium-low heat 10 - 12 minutes, or until livers lose pink color. Remove from heat and let cool 10 minutes.

In a food processor using steel blade, puree liver mixture. Add salt, pepper, mustard, butter and brandy and process until smooth.

Spoon into a crock and either eat immediately, or store, covered in refrigerator. Très good, spread on freshly baked French bread, sesame crackers or apple slices.

OOOOO... LA-LA!

BEEF BOURGUIGNON (FANCY BEEF STEW)

Chunks of beef cooked forever in a hearty
stock and topped with tender mushrooms.

Serves 6

3 slices bacon
1/2 cup chopped onions (about 1 medium onion)
2 cloves garlic, minced
1/2 cup flour
2 teaspoons salt
1/2 teaspoon pepper
3 pound beef chuck roast, cut into 2" cubes
1 cup beef stock or broth
3 cups Burgundy wine
1 bay leaf
1/2 teaspoon ground thyme
1 teaspoon sugar
2 tablespoons cornstarch dissolved in 3 tablespoons cold
water
1/2 pound small mushrooms, trimmed
3 tablespoons butter or margarine

In a large, heavy skillet with a lid, cook bacon until crisp. Remove bacon, and in the bacon fat, cook onion and garlic until golden. Remove from skillet and set aside.

In a shallow bowl, mix flour with salt and pepper. Dredge meat chunks in seasoned flour and brown meat in the bacon grease. If you need to, add a tablespoon or two of vegetable oil to the skillet to keep meat from sticking. When meat is browned, add to the skillet the beef stock, wine, bay leaf, thyme, sugar and the cooked onion. Crumble the bacon over the top, and stir the stew. Bring to a boil, turn heat to low, cover tightly and simmer 3 hours. Give it a stir every now and then. Remove bay leaf and discard. Stir in dissolved cornstarch to thicken the broth.

Just before serving, cook mushrooms in butter in a small skillet about 4 minutes. Ladle stew into big bowls and top with mushrooms.

FRENCH LETTUCE SALAD (FANCY MIXED GREENS)

*French salads are typically simple, so as not to compete
with other courses - so here it is, a simple, refreshing salad.*

Serves 6

Dressing:
1/3 cup olive oil (extra virgin is preferable)
2 tablespoons white wine vinegar
1/2 teaspoon salt
1/4 teaspoon freshly ground black pepper
1 tablespoon prepared brown mustard
1 clove garlic, minced

1 small head Boston lettuce
1/2 small head romaine lettuce
6 leaves red leaf lettuce

Make dressing: Put all dressing ingredients in a jar with a screw-on lid. Shake well and refrigerate.

Rinse all lettuces in cold water. Tear into bite-sized pieces and wrap in a tea towel. Refrigerate.

To serve: Place lettuce mixture in a large bowl, pour dressing over, and toss to coat.

GRILLED FRENCH BREAD with BRIE BUTTER (FANCY TOAST and CHEESE)

French bread topped with a tomato-Brie
spread and grilled until perfectly bronzed.

Serves 6

1/4 pound soft, ripened Brie cheese
1/2 cup (1 stick) butter or margarine
2 tablespoons tomato paste
3 cloves garlic, finely minced
1/2 loaf fresh, French bread

Preheat oven to 375 degrees.

Place Brie, butter, tomato paste and garlic in a food processor with a steel blade. Process until smooth, scraping often. Slice the piece of French bread in half lengthwise and spread the Brie butter on the cut side. Bake 15 minutes or until cheese is browned and bubbly. Serve warm. French bread stales very quickly, so use the leftover half to make croutons.

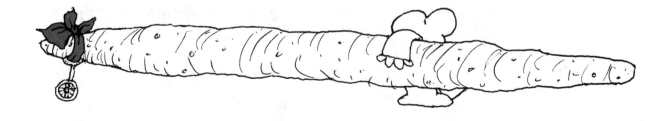

DOUBLE DARK CHOCOLATE MOUSSE
(FANCY CHOCOLATE PUDDING)

The sweetened whipped cream is a must for this bordering-on-bitter chocolate treat. Also, because the eggs are not cooked, make sure you get them fresh, from a reliable source.

Serves 6

4 ounces semi-sweet chocolate
3 ounces unsweetened chocolate
3 tablespoons brewed coffee
5 eggs, separated
1 cup heavy whipping cream
3 tablespoons sugar

In the top of a double boiler over low heat, put both chocolates and the brewed coffee. Cook, stirring, until melted. Add egg yolks and mix well. Remove from heat and let cool slightly.

Using an electric mixer, beat egg whites until stiff. Fold whites into chocolate mixture. Spoon into individual serving cups and chill at least 1 1/2 hours.

Beat cream and sugar together with an electric mixer until whipped. Top each serving of mousse with a generous spoonful of whipped cream. Your craving for chocolate will be satisfied for quite some time.

Chapter 20

MOMMA MIA'S ITALIAN FEAST

A celebration of Italian treats ... a feast for the eyes as well as the stomach.

OH! SO BUCCO!

Veal shanks, cooked in an aromatic broth along with a variety of garden vegetables. This was once a Milanese peasants dish, but became so popular, it can now be found in some of the finest restaurants (or diners) in the world.

Serves 4 - 6

6 veal shank steaks, 2" thick (about 4 pounds)
1/4 cup flour, seasoned with a little salt and pepper
5 tablespoons olive oil
6 tablespoons butter or margarine
2 medium onions, coarsely chopped
1/4 cup chopped shallots
3 cloves garlic, minced
1 1/2 cups diced carrots (about 6)
1 1/2 cups chopped zucchini
1/2 cup white wine
1 cup beef stock or broth
14 1/2 ounce can Italian plum tomatoes, drained and coarsely chopped
2 teaspoons chopped fresh parsley (or 1/2 teaspoon dried)
1 tablespoon chopped fresh basil (or 1 teaspoon dried)
1 teaspoon salt
1/2 teaspoon pepper

IT'S OH, SO GOOD !!

217

Coat each veal shank generously in seasoned flour. Heat oil in a large, deep skillet and, over medium heat, brown shanks on both sides (15 - 20 minutes). Remove to a plate. Drain oil, leaving the brown bits on the bottom of the pan. Melt butter in skillet and add onions, shallots and garlic. Cook until golden. Add carrots and zucchini and cook 5 minutes more. Pour wine and beef stock over vegetables and bring to a simmer, stirring. Return veal shanks to skillet and add tomatoes and spices. Lower heat and simmer 2 hours, covered. Serve with rice or pasta to soak up the wonderful juices.

SPAGHETTI with BOLOGNESE SAUCE

One of the most wonderful of all Italian meat sauces and just a nice change from your regular spaghetti sauce. Filled with finely chopped carrots and onions, ground pork and beef, wine, beef stock and cream.

Serves 6

2 tablespoons olive oil
1/4 pound prociutto, finely chopped (or 4 slices bacon,
        finely chopped)
1 medium onion, finely chopped
2 medium carrots, scraped and finely chopped
2 celery ribs, finely chopped
2 cloves garlic, minced
3/4 pound ground beef round or sirloin
1/2 pound ground pork
1/2 cup Marsala wine, divided
2 cups beef stock or broth, divided
6 ounce can tomato paste

            1 teaspoon salt
        1/2 teaspoon pepper
        1/2 teaspoon dried parsley
        1/4 teaspoon dried basil
        1/2 cup heavy cream
            1 pound thin spaghetti, cooked according to package
                    directions
        Freshly grated Parmesan cheese

In a large, deep skillet, heat olive oil. Over medium heat, cook prosciutto until lightly browned, about 3 minutes. Add onion, carrots, celery and garlic and cook, stirring, until onion is softened. Break up ground beef and pork and add to skillet. Cook until pink has disappeared, about 10 minutes. Add half the wine and half the beef stock. Cook over medium-high heat until liquid is almost absorbed, about 15 minutes. Lower heat, stir in tomato paste, salt, pepper, parsley, and basil. Pour in remaining wine and beef stock. Simmer, covered, 20 minutes. Stir in the cream and heat through. Spoon sauce over a mountain of tender spaghetti noodles and pass the cheese around.

GRANDMAMA'S SUCCOTASH

An Italian version of the ultimate grandmother's vegetable dish. Featuring plum tomatoes, fresh corn and cannelini beans in a flavorful cream sauce.

Serves 6 - 8

3 tablespoons butter or margarine
1 Spanish onion, chopped
2 cloves garlic, minced
28 ounce can Italian plum tomatoes, drained and coarsely
    chopped
1 tablespoon chopped fresh basil (or 1/2 teaspoon dried)
1/2 teaspoon dry mustard
2 cups fresh, cooked corn kernels (or 10 ounce frozen
    package, thawed)
19 ounce can cannelini beans, drained
2 teaspoons cider vinegar
1/2 teaspoon salt
1/2 teaspoon pepper
1/2 cup heavy cream

Melt butter in a large skillet. Add onion and garlic and cook over medium heat 5 minutes, or until onion is soft. Stir in tomatoes, tarragon and mustard. Add corn, cannelini beans, vinegar, salt and pepper. Cover and cook over low heat 10 - 15 minutes. Just before serving, stir in cream and heat through.

GRILLED ANTIPASTO BREAD

Fresh Italian bread, spread with tomato butter that's mixed with bits of olives and Genoa salami, topped with mozzarella and baked until bubbly.

Serves 6

1/2 cup (1 stick) sweet butter, softened
1 tablespoon tomato paste
1/2 cup finely chopped Genoa salami (about 8 slices)
2 tablespoons chopped black olives
1 teaspoon chopped fresh oregano (or 1/4 teaspoon dried)
1/4 pound Mozzarella cheese, sliced
1 loaf fresh Italian bread, halved lengthwise

Preheat oven to 450 degrees.

In a medium bowl, mash together butter and tomato paste with a fork until creamy. Fold in salami, olives and oregano. Spread butter mixture on cut sides of bread and place on baking sheet, butter side up. Bake 10 minutes.

Remove bread from oven and turn oven to broil. Arrange cheese slices over buttered bread and return to oven. Broil until cheese is lightly browned. You could even serve this as an appetizer.

DON'T YOU EVER WANT TO DO ANYTHING BUT LOAF AROUND?

ITALIAN RICE with FRESH PEAS and PARMESAN CHEESE

*Risotto, simmered in chicken stock until fluffy and decorated
with fresh, sweet peas and freshly grated Parmesan cheese.*

Serves 4 - 6

2 tablespoons olive oil
2 tablespoons butter or margarine
1 large onion, finely chopped
2 cups Italian rice (Arborio)
4 cups chicken stock or broth, divided
2 tablespoons sweet butter, softened
2 cups fresh shelled peas
3/4 cup freshly grated Parmesan cheese
1 teaspoon salt
1/2 teaspoon pepper

In a large saucepan, heat oil and butter. Cook onion until soft. Stir in rice and 2 cups of the chicken stock. Bring to a boil and simmer, uncovered, until liquid is almost absorbed, stirring frequently. Add remaining 2 cups chicken stock, sweet butter and peas and simmer 15 more minutes. Stir in cheese, salt and pepper. Test rice for doneness before serving.

NOW, YOUNG MAN, I INSIST, YOU EAT EVERY GRAIN OF RICE, AND PEA ON YOUR PLATE!

CHOCOLATE RICOTTA CREAM PUFFS

*A variation of the popular cannoli. Airy puffs of pastry,
stuffed with the most wonderful chocolate filling.*

Makes 12 - 14 (allow 2 per person)

Pastry:

    1 cup water
    1/2 cup (1 stick) butter or margarine
    1 cup flour
    4 eggs

    3 squares (1 ounce each) semi-sweet chocolate
    1 square (1 ounce) unsweetened chocolate
    15 ounce tub traditional ricotta cheese
    3 tablespoons sugar
    Confectioners' sugar for dusting

Make pastry: Preheat oven to 400 degrees. In a medium saucepan over medium heat, simmer water with butter until butter melts. Remove from heat, and all at once, stir flour in. Return to low heat and cook, stirring, until mixture leaves sides of pan. Remove from heat again, and beat eggs in, one at a time, with a wooden spoon until batter is shiny.

Drop by heaping tablespoonfuls onto ungreased baking sheet and bake 25 - 30 minutes, or until golden. Let cool.

Meanwhile, make filling: Melt both chocolates in the top of a double boiler over hot, not boiling water. Let cool.

In a large bowl, beat the ricotta cheese with the sugar using an electric mixer until smooth and creamy. Fold in cooled chocolate.

To assemble: Slice the tops off the pastry puffs. Pinch out any excess dough from the puffs. Fill each one with the chocolate-ricotta mixture and place tops back on. Just before serving, sift confectioners' sugar over the tops. Store in refrigerator.

ORANGE-CRANBERRY ICE

Hold each spoonful on your tongue and let the flavor just trickle down your throat. Refreshing after a hearty plate of pasta.

Serves 8

1 cup water
1/2 cup sugar
1 1/2 cups fresh orange juice, strained
1/2 cup frozen cranberry juice concentrate

In a large saucepan, mix water with sugar. Bring to a boil and cook 5 minutes. Remove from heat and let cool.

Mix orange juice and cranberry juice concentrate with cooled sugar syrup. Transfer to a gallon-size plastic food storage bag. Place on baking sheet and freeze several hours, turning bag occasionally. It should be served frozen, but somewhat soft. If it hardens, whirl it in the food processor.

You are invited to a surprise birthday party for
Ziggy at my place. Please bring a dish to share
... I'll bake the cake.

Mom

Chapter 21

SURPRISE BIRTHDAY PARTY FOR ZIGGY

HERMAN'S NO-FAIL STORE-BOUGHT ONION DIP
with CHIPS

Serves: How ever many the package says

1 tub onion dip
1 large bag potato chips

Peel top off onion dip container. Transfer chips to a bowl. Eat.

CHARLIE BROWN'S PLAIN OLD CHICKEN FINGERS
with PEANUTS DIP

It's nothing too fancy - predictable chicken pieces,
breaded and baked - but the dip is kind of special.

© 1950 United Feature Syndicate, Inc.

Makes about 55

3 1/2 pounds boneless, skinless chicken breast,
partially frozen for easier slicing
1/2 cup milk
2 teaspoons salt
5 eggs, beaten
2 1/2 cups Italian-style seasoned dry bread crumbs
1 cup (2 sticks) butter or margarine

Peanuts dip:
1 medium onion, finely chopped (about 1 cup)
1 tablespoon vegetable oil
1/4 teaspoon cayenne pepper
1 cup tomato juice
2/3 cup peanut butter

Slice chicken into strips about 1" x 2". Place in a large glass bowl.
Combine milk and salt and pour over chicken, turning to coat. Cover and
refrigerate 1 hour.

Preheat oven to 375 degrees.

Place eggs in a shallow bowl. Place bread crumbs in another shallow bowl. Coat chicken pieces in bread crumbs, then eggs, then bread crumbs again.

Put butter in either one extra large roasting pan, or divide between two regular-sized ones. Melt butter in the oven and then remove.

Place coated chicken pieces in melted butter and turn to coat. Bake, uncovered, 40 minutes or until golden brown.

Meanwhile, make Peanuts dip: In a medium saucepan, cook onions in oil over medium heat until softened. Add cayenne pepper, tomato juice and peanut butter. Cook and stir until warm and smooth. Serve immediately with baked chicken fingers.

BLONDIE'S DAGWOOD PARTY SANDWICH

A mountainous triple-layered round bread loaf, seasoned with mustard butter, piled high with turkey and corned beef, and overflowing with all the trimmings expected in a true Dagwood sandwich.

Serves 8 - 10 (if Dagwood's not around)

1 large, round loaf of crusty white bread
6 tablespoons sweet butter, softened
2 - 3 tablespoons prepared brown mustard
1/2 pound corned beef, thinly sliced
1/4 pound Swiss cheese, thinly sliced
1 medium tomato, thinly sliced
1/2 pound turkey breast, thinly sliced
3 hard-boiled eggs, sliced
Several leaves of lettuce

Slice bread into 3 layers. In a small bowl, mix together butter and mustard. Spread a third of the mustard-butter on the bottom bread layer. Top with half the corned beef, Swiss cheese, tomato, turkey, egg slices and lettuce, in that order. Place middle layer of bread on top. Use another third of the mustard-butter on that layer, and repeat with remaining ingredients. Spread the rest of the mustard-butter on the cut side of the last bread layer and press down gently. Wrap sandwich tightly in plastic wrap and refrigerate until serving time. Cut into pie-shaped wedges.

EUGENE'S JUMBO BARBECUED SHRIMP

Peel and eat shrimp - coated in such a scrumptiously tangy sauce, I guarantee you won't forget it. Have plenty of napkins on hand.

Makes 50 - 60 pieces

1/3 cup olive oil
3 cloves garlic, minced
1/4 cup soy sauce
1/4 cup ketchup
1/4 teaspoon ground ginger
1/2 teaspoon ground cumin
1/4 teaspoon coriander
1/2 teaspoon cayenne pepper
2 pounds jumbo, green (uncooked) shrimp

In a large bowl, whisk together all ingredients except the shrimp. Add shrimp (don't peel), and toss to coat. Let stand 10 minutes.

Pour shrimp and sauce into a large skillet, and cook over medium-hot heat until pink, about 4 - 5 minutes, turning. You can also place them on a grill to cook, basting them with the sauce. Serve with animal crackers.

231

WIZARD OF ID'S MAGIC DISAPPEARING MEAT PIES

*Individual pork and beef pies, surrounded by tender pastry
and capped with tomato-mashed potatoes. Three easy
steps using muffin tins to form the pie shells. Royal fare!*

Makes about 40

Pastry:

8 ounce package cream cheese, softened
1 cup (2 sticks) butter, softened
1/2 teaspoon salt
2 cups flour

Filling:

2 tablespoons vegetable oil
1 small onion, chopped
3/4 pound ground beef chuck
1/4 pound ground pork
2 cloves garlic, minced
1 teaspoon salt
1/4 teaspoon cayenne pepper

Topping:

3 large potatoes, peeled and chunked
2 tablespoons butter or margarine
1/4 cup milk
2 tablespoons tomato paste

232

Make pastry: In a large bowl, mix together pastry ingredients with hands. Form into a large patio, wrap in plastic wrap and refrigerate one hour to firm it up for rolling.

Meanwhile, make filling: In a large skillet, heat vegetable oil and cook onion over medium heat until soft. Add both meats and cook until done, breaking up with a fork. Stir in garlic, salt and cayenne. Set aside.

Make topping: Steam potatoes until tender, about 15 minutes. While hot, add butter and milk and beat with an electric mixer until smooth. Fold in tomato paste. Stir about 1/3 of the potato mixture into the meat filling.

Preheat oven to 375 degrees. Cut chilled pastry dough into two pieces. On a floured surface, roll dough out to 1/8" thickness. Cut 3" circles using cookie cutter or drinking glass. Place rounds in muffin tins, and press down, forming a small edge to hold the filling. Bake, unfilled 20 minutes or until lightly golden.

Remove from oven, place about 1 tablespoon of meat filling in each pastry and top with a spoonful of potato-tomato mixture. Return meat pies to oven and bake 10 minutes more, or until heated through. Watch them disappear.

POOF

ALA.
KA·ZOT

HAGAR'S HORRIBLE HAM

*A terribly delicious raspberry-mustard glazed ham that should
be served Viking-style: after it cools down a little from the oven,
place it on a platter with a couple of sharp knives, and have guests
carve their own pieces right off the bone and eat it with their fingers.*

Serves a small village

8 pound semi-boneless cooked ham half
3 tablespoons prepared brown mustard
3 tablespoons raspberry jam
1 teaspoon lime juice
3 tablespoons brown sugar
1 tablespoon black pepper
1 tablespoon light cream or half and half
3 tablespoons dry red wine

Preheat oven to 375 degrees. Prepare ham by making several long slits lengthwise down the ham, about 1/2" deep. Place in a large roasting pan.

In a small bowl, combine remaining ingredients and mix well. Brush about half the glaze on ham. Bake 1 1/2 hours, uncovered, basting two more times with the rest of the glaze. Fetch the ale.

234

BEETLE BAILEY'S MUSHROOMS on a SHINGLE

Toast points covered with a delicious, fresh mushroom spread. Army food at its finest (when Cookie allows me in his kitchen, that is).

Makes 56

4 tablespoons sweet butter
3 tablespoons finely chopped shallots
1 1/2 pounds fresh mushrooms; washed, trimmed and chopped
1 tablespoon dried tarragon leaves
1 tablespoon dried oregano leaves
3 tablespoons flour
1 1/2 teaspoons salt
1/3 cup heavy cream
14 slices white bread

© 1993. Reprinted with special permission of King Features Syndicate.

In a large skillet over medium heat, melt butter. Add shallots and cook until softened. Stir in mushrooms, tarragon and oregano and cook until mushrooms are tender. Sprinkle flour over and cook another minute or two, stirring, until flour is absorbed. Pour cream in and mix well. Simmer until mixture is thickened.

Preheat oven to broil. Place bread slices on baking sheets and broil until one side is golden brown. Remove from oven, turn slices over and spread unbrowned side with mushroom mixture. Return to oven and broil until heated through and bubbly. Cut each into four triangles and serve warm. Leave the dishes for Cookie.

MARY WORTH'S ATOMIC MEATBALLS

Who says I'm not part of the nuclear age? My triple-pepper meatballs will set your mouth ablaze. Of course, they're served with a side of soothing Sweet and Sour Tomato Sauce. And, the sensible side of me has made them square (no rolling necessary).

Makes 75

4 slices white bread, softened in a little water and
    squeezed dry
3 pounds ground beef sirloin
2 eggs
1/3 cup finely chopped onion
2 teaspoons ground white pepper
2 teaspoons black pepper
2 1/2 teaspoons cayenne pepper
1 1/2 teaspoons salt

Tomato sauce: 1 cup crushed tomatoes in puree (from a can)
3 tablespoons lemon juice
1 tablespoon brown sugar
1 tablespoon sugar
1 tablespoon sour cream
1/4 teaspoon salt

236

Make meatballs: Preheat oven to 375 degrees.

In a very large bowl, combine softened bread, ground beef, eggs, onion, all the peppers and the salt. Spread mixture evenly in a 9" x 13" roasting pan. Bake 45 minutes (meat will shrink slightly). Remove from oven and let cool slightly. Cut into 1" squares and transfer to a serving bowl or plate. Have toothpicks available.

While meatballs are cooking, make Sweet and Sour Tomato Sauce: Put all ingredients in a food processor with a steel blade. Process until smooth. Serve in a bowl next to the meatballs.

SAUNDERS
AND
GIELLA

SNOOPY'S CHOCOLATE CHERRY BARK

*Rich, dark chocolate and chewy dried cherries -
such a yummy treat it makes me want to dance.*

Makes 1 dog dishful

13 squares (1 ounce each) semi-sweet chocolate
3 squares (1 ounce each) unsweetened chocolate
3 ounces pitted, dried bing cherries (about 3/4 cup)

In the top of a double boiler over hot, not boiling water, melt both chocolates. Remove from heat.

Cut up the dried cherries into little pieces with kitchen scissors. Stir into the melted chocolate. Spread the bark about 1/8" thick onto a sheet of waxed paper and let harden. Break into pieces before serving. Store, tightly covered, in a cool place.

Note: I once gave some to Lucy and she liked me for awhile.

GARFIELD'S CHICKEN LASAGNA ROLL-UPS

*Cool, creamy chicken salad with apple, walnuts and sage
rolled up inside my favorite noodle. Great paw food.*

Makes about 40

2 pounds boneless, skinless chicken breast (2 large)
1 pound lasagna noodles
1 cup mayonnaise
1 tablespoon chopped fresh sage leaves
    (or 1/2 teaspoon dried)
1 teaspoon salt
1/2 teaspoon lemon pepper
1/3 cup chopped walnuts
1/2 apple, peeled and grated

GARFIELD: © 1978 United Feature Syndicate

Toss the chicken in a large saucepan with some water and boil until tender, about 20 - 25 minutes, or the time it takes for a short nap. Drain and let cool.

In a large pot, cook lasagna noodles according to package directions. Rinse thoroughly in cold water and drain. Set aside.

Break chicken into small pieces and ship any scraps overnight freight to me. Place chicken in a large bowl with the rest of the ingredients and mix well. Taste for seasoning. Taste again to be certain. Taste once more.
Cut cooked lasagna noodles in half widthwise, place about 1 tablespoon filling on each noodle piece, and roll up. Sprinkle tops with a little lemon pepper. I prefer a dusting of catnip, however.

EL'S BETTER WURST

Bratwurst cooked in beer, sliced, and then coated with a mustard-cherry glaze. Perfect for a busy mother because it's easy, it makes a lot, and it's wonderfully tangy.

Makes about 60 pieces

2 1/2 pounds bratwurst (about 10)
  12 ounce beer
1/2 cup prepared brown mustard
1/2 cup cherry jelly
1/2 teaspoon pepper

Place bratwurst in a large skillet. Pour beer over. Bring to a boil, let the dog out, lower heat and simmer, uncovered, 40 minutes, turning once.

Meanwhile, change the laundry, vacuum the living room, empty the wastebaskets and put away all the stuff that's accumulated on the stairs.

If beer evaporates, add more as needed. When brats start to brown, remove from heat and cut into bite-sized pieces, right in the pan. Answer the phone. Pour fat off.

In a small saucepan, combine mustard, cherry jelly and pepper and cook over low heat until jelly melts. Pour this mixture over the bratwurst pieces and toss thoroughly. Simmer until heated through. Serve warm with toothpicks.

Take a long, hot, soothing bath before the party.

CRANKSHAFT'S CRABBY DIP

Everyone on the block has been after me for years for my famous dip. Well, if you promise to quit bothering me, here it is: a favorite hot artichoke dip, made better with crab meat and sherry.

Serves half a bus load

14 ounce can artichoke hearts, drained
1 cup mayonnaise
1 cup Parmesan cheese (the kind in the can)
2 cloves garlic, minced
2 tablespoons dry sherry
6 1/2 ounce can good quality crab meat, drained
Butter crackers

Preheat oven to 425 degrees. Chop artichokes and place in a large bowl. Stir in mayonnaise, cheese, garlic and sherry. Fold in crab meat. Dump mixture in a one-quart casserole dish.

Bake, uncovered, 20 minutes or until top is browned. Now leave me alone.

Chapter 22

HOT COCOA BEFORE BEDTIME

This richly sweet and soothing hot chocolate tastes best just after that first yawn of the evening.....or on a Sunday afternoon after a ride on the neighborhood sledding hill.

ABOUT THE CREATORS OF THIS BOOK

Robin Benzle is the author of the critically acclaimed *COOKING WITH HUMOR*. She also writes humor/food articles for such publications as *The Cleveland Plain Dealer* and *The Los Angeles Times Syndicate*; and enjoys teaching and entertaining through television, radio and public appearances. She is a Mom to two daughters, Bailey and Erin, and together with her husband, Eric, lives and cooks in Bay Village, Ohio.

Tom Wilson is the Emmy award-winning creative mind behind Ziggy, America's best-loved Everyman. Ziggy began life over 20 years ago as a comic strip, and today is read by over 100 million people in every major US city in daily and Sunday newspapers. He is syndicated in 20 countries, from Finland to the Philippines, and everyone, at one time or another, has probably received a Ziggy greeting card. He lives and eats pot roast in Lakewood, Ohio (Tom Wilson, not Ziggy).

Together, they have combined their talents and love of good home cooking to bring Mom's Diner to life for your cooking and eating pleasure.